Gastric Sleeve Cookbook

Nutritious Early Post-Operative Bariatric Recipes to Maintain Your Weight & Control It Easily

By

PENELOPE HAYNES

© **Copyright 2023 by PENELOPE HAYNES - All rights reserved.**

This document is geared towards providing exact and reliable information in regards to the topic and issue covered. The publication is sold with the idea that the publisher is not required to render accounting, officially permitted, or otherwise, qualified services. If advice is necessary, legal or professional, a practiced individual in the profession should be ordered.

- From a Declaration of Principles which was accepted and approved equally by a Committee of the American Bar Association and a Committee of Publishers and Associations.

In no way is it legal to reproduce, duplicate, or transmit any part of this document in either electronic means or in printed format. Recording of this publication is strictly prohibited, and any storage of this document is not allowed unless with written permission from the publisher. All rights reserved.

The information provided herein is stated to be truthful and consistent, in that any liability, in terms of inattention or otherwise, by any usage or abuse of any policies, processes, or directions contained within is the solitary and utter responsibility of the recipient reader. Under no circumstances will any legal responsibility or blame be held against the publisher for any reparation, damages, or monetary loss due to the information herein, either directly or indirectly.

Respective authors own all copyrights not held by the publisher.

The information herein is offered for informational purposes solely and is universal as so. The presentation of the information is without a contract or any type of guarantee assurance.

The trademarks used are without any consent, and the trademark publication is without permission or backing by the trademark owner. All trademarks and brands within this book are for clarifying purposes only and are owned by the owners, not affiliated with this document.

Table of Contents

Introduction **5**

Chapter 1 Gastric Sleeve Surgery **7**
   1.1 Overview of Gastric Sleeve Surgery....7
   1.2 Pre-Operative Diet.......................... 9
   1.3 Stages of the postoperative diet 12
   1.4 Advice and Recommendations...........17

Chapter 2 Early Post-Operative Diet 18
   2.1 Soymilk Shake..................................18
   2.2 Mango Pineapple Shake 18
   2.3 Soupy Chicken 19
   2.4 Chicken Squash 20
   2.5 Mixed Berries Shake....................... 22
   2.6 Vanilla Shake.................................. 23
   2.7 Choco mint Milkshake 23
   2.8 Pea Pottage..................................... 24
   2.9 Creamy Carrot Soup 25
   2.10 Hearty Tomato 26
   2.11 Double Fudge Chocolate Shake 27
   2.12 Peanut Butter Cup Shake 28
   2.13 Mango Smoothie............................ 28
   2.14 Classic Tuna Salad 29
   2.15 Chicken Salad............................... 30
   2.16 Fried Beans 31
   2.17 Superfood Smoothie...................... 32
   2.18 Apple Pie Shake 33
   2.19 Super Soup 33
   2.20 Creamy Smoothie.......................... 34

Chapter 3 Breakfast Recipes 36
   3.1 Blueberry Pancakes 36
   3.2 Peach Smoothie 37
   3.3 Chicken Tart 38
   3.4 Apple Avocado Juice 39

3.5 Scrambler Egg 39
3.6 Pumpkin Latte 41
3.7 Radish Hash................................... 42
3.8 Chicken Pineapple Skewers 42
3.9 Bacon Eggy Bites............................ 43
3.10 Greek Omelet................................ 44
3.11 Zucchini Hash 45
3.12 Classic Enchiladas 45
3.13 Fruits Oat 46
3.14 Savory Soufflé 48
3.15 Salmon Bruschetta........................ 49
3.16 Pecan Pikelets 50
3.17 Acorn Squash 51
3.18 Cinnamon Chiller.......................... 52
3.19 Sweet Potato Waffles 53
3.20 Veggies Cupcakes 54

Chapter 4 Vegetarian Recipes.......... 56
   4.1 Bean Wraps.................................... 56
   4.2 Roasted Eggplant 57
   4.3 Balsamic Veggies............................58
   4.4 Roasted Cauliflower 59
   4.5 Broccoli Rabe 60
   4.6 Fried Wok Veggies.......................... 61
   4.7 BBQ Vegetables.............................. 62
   4.8 Barley Lentil Soup 63
   4.9 Mushroom Basil Soup 64
   4.10 Mixed Skillet................................. 65
   4.11 Wild Rice Salad 66
   4.12 Curried Veggies............................ 67
   4.13 Spicy Tofu.................................... 69
   4.14 Zucchini Noodles.......................... 70
   4.15 Pinto Beans...................................71

Chapter 5 Poultry Recipes 73
- 5.1 Baked Potato Soup 73
- 5.2 Creamy Chicken Soup 74
- 5.3 Barley Veggie Chicken Soup 75
- 5.4 Grilled Chicken Wings 76
- 5.5 Mexican Taco Skillet 77
- 5.6 Turkey Meatloaf 78
- 5.7 Zucchini and Turkey Meatloaf 80
- 5.8 Chicken Cordon Bleu 82
- 5.9 Egg Roll 83
- 5.10 Chicken with Mango Salsa 84

Chapter 6 Sides and Snacks 87
- 6.1 Tuna Sandwich 87
- 6.2 Steak Fajita 88
- 6.3 Fruity Solace 90
- 6.4 Mashed Cauliflower 90
- 6.5 Pickle Roll-ups 91
- 6.6 Butternut Puree 92
- 6.7 Zucchini Fries 92
- 6.8 Eggplant Pizzas 93
- 6.9 Mixed Salad 94
- 6.10 Chipotle Hummus 95

Chapter 7 Beef & Pork Recipes 97
- 7.1 Pork Tenderloin Balsamic 97
- 7.2 Easy Meatloaf 98
- 7.3 Black Bean with Pork Verde Stew ... 98
- 7.4 Beef Stir Fry 99
- 7.5 Chipotle Pork 101
- 7.6 Beef Stew 102

Chapter 8 Desserts 104
- 8.1 Chocolate Chia Pudding 104
- 8.2 Peanut Butter Cookies 105
- 8.3 Berry Custard 106
- 8.4 Fruity Jelly Wrap 107
- 8.5 Peanut Butter Pancakes 108

Chapter 9 30 Days Meal Plan 109
- Week 1 109
- Week 2 110
- Week 3 111
- Week 4 111
- Week 5 112

Conclusion 113

Introduction

When you are at the point where you are ready to explore bariatric surgery, you have tried all there is to do to lose weight. You have tried every conceivable diet, including juicing fasts consisting entirely of soup, diets low in carbohydrates, diets rich in protein, and diets low in Fat. You are an authority on various weight reduction diets. You may have shed some weight, but it doesn't seem like it will stay. It has the potential to make you question your mental health and well-being. What are you doing that other people aren't? How are you different?

The World Obesity Federation thinks obesity ought to be regarded as an illness, even though it does not satisfy the scientific definition of a disease. It is a chronic condition that worsens progressively over time, and patients might have relapses even after losing weight. Certain physiological changes occur in the body when you acquire weight, encouraging more weight gain. When we are hungry, our insulin levels and the hormones that warn us we are hungry go up. And levels of our satiety hormones decline, which makes us want to eat more than we normally would.

Alterations to one's diet and way of life seem to be effective in reversing these alterations for most individuals. They adjust their eating habits, begin an exercise routine, and then go on with their lives after seeing weight loss. However, for other people, maintaining weight control becomes an ongoing battle. These individuals need to adopt a different approach, one that is more medical. One may include medication and bariatric surgery as part of the treatment plan.

It is important to note that bariatric surgery is not a cosmetic operation. It is for persons whose weight and body fat are causing them to have health problems. Important improvements in underlying metabolic health issues, such as cardiovascular disease and diabetes, are one of the most significant advantages that may result from a substantial reduction in body mass.

Making that choice is not going to be simple at all. After all, it is likely that throughout your life, you have been taught that the only thing you need to do is cut down on the amount of food you consume and increase the amount of physical activity you perform. However, after several years of attempting that treatment with little success, you have concluded that it is time to take responsibility for your and your surgeon's health. If you are reading this, it means that you have either decided to take action or have already done so and are prepared to go on to the next phase. Well done!

This is not simply another attempt at losing weight. You are putting a lot of effort into improving your health. You have decided to undergo the necessary but very nerve-wracking bariatric surgery procedure. Now that it's over, you need to determine whether or not it was worthwhile. The time has come to begin our true labor. If you don't support the treatment with the appropriate diet and eating routine, it won't be able to provide you with effects that last over the long term. The recipes in this book will take you from the time after surgery when you are restricted to a liquid diet, through the time when you are restricted to a diet of pureed foods to the time when you are restricted to a diet of soft foods, and beyond, all the while promoting your overall health and helping you to maintain the weight loss you have achieved.

Chapter 1 Gastric Sleeve Surgery

Everyone aims to improve their health and shed excess weight to seem more intelligent and alluring. Bariatric surgery, also known as gastric sleeve surgery, is a procedure that involves making the stomach smaller to facilitate weight loss. You will be provided comprehensive information on the procedure in the subsequent parts of this guide.

1.1 Overview of Gastric Sleeve Surgery

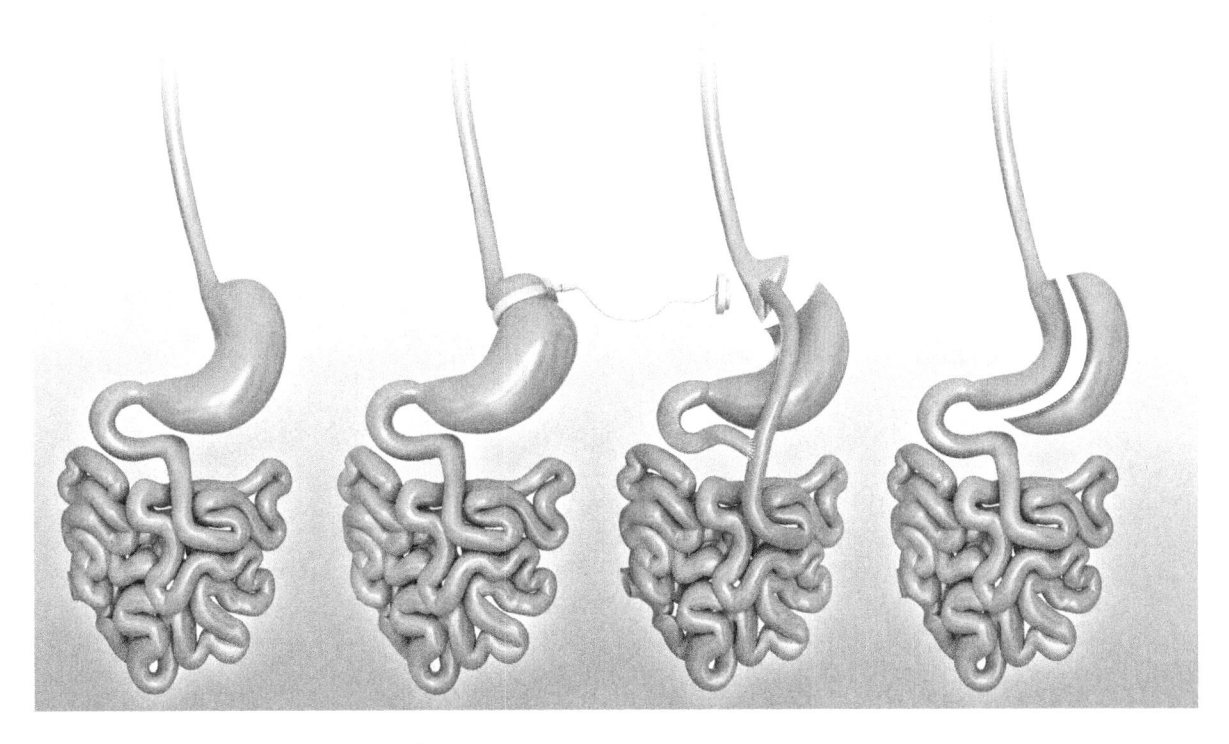

Patients looking for excellent weight loss in a direct method that does not require the maintenance and long-haul intricacy rates of a lap band have found that gastric sleeve surgery, also known as sleeve gastrectomy, has become a popular option in recent years. This procedure is also known as sleeve gastrectomy.

A gastric sleeve is a surgical procedure that permanently lowers the size of your stomach by 66 percent. It is used as a weight loss technique. Laparoscopic sleeve gastrectomy is the name given to the procedure that is carried out via an incision the size of a keyhole. A small incision is created in your stomach, which reduces the amount of scarring and shortens the time needed to recover after surgery. The expert will use this incision to insert the laparoscope and any other surgical tools necessary.

When having part of the contents of your stomach removed, the remaining area of your stomach will be stapled shut after the procedure is complete. The operation is carried out while the patient is under the influence of a general anesthetic, and after about one month, they can resume their normal activities. This weight loss method is irreversible, unlike other weight loss operations such as stomach banding. It does not involve the implantation of any external materials, as with gastric bands.

Because you will be eating less, the food you consume must provide you with the nutrients and vitamins your body needs. How exactly does this kind of weight reduction surgery work to benefit patients?

This technique limits the stomach's capacity, making it easier for you to experience feelings of fullness and satisfaction after eating.

In addition, the removal of the majority of the stomach results in a reduction in the level of the hormone ghrelin. This, in turn, reduces cravings and enables patients to feel less hungry in the time between meals.

As a result, the patient will consume fewer calories overall, which will help them achieve their weight loss goals.

Who is it that may stand to gain from using this approach?

You could be a good candidate for a gastric sleeve if you are severely obese, have a body mass index (BMI) of 40, or have a BMI of 35 or more and have exhausted all other possibilities to be in better condition. Every patient is evaluated to determine whether or not they are healthy enough to have surgery and whether or not they have a complete understanding of the risks and responsibilities associated with the treatment.

Can you tell me why it could be a good idea to consider having surgery to help me lose weight?

Excess weight is a key contributor to feelings of hopelessness, increased anxiety, and less social recognition, and it has a detrimental influence on a person's appearance and demeanor. A sleeve gastrectomy is performed to bring the patient's weight down to a more manageable range. This is done in the hopes that the bulk of the problems associated with obesity would improve or go away, leading to a more contented presence.

If you are morbidly obese and conventional weight management methods are not working for you, laparoscopic sleeve gastrectomy may assist you in making a full recovery.

1.2 Pre-Operative Diet

This part will cover the five measures that will help you prepare for bariatric surgery most effectively. This will explain how to effectively manage the postoperative period and plan your diet to lose weight healthily and keep it off for good.

If, on the other hand, you have not yet had surgery, you should continue reading this part. In this section, you will discover all the information you need to take the appropriate care of your body in preparation for the process. But before we get into it, let's look at the advantages of adhering to these five measures before your operation. Improve the method such that it is both safer and simpler. Fat deposits surrounding the liver will be easier for the surgeon to remove if you follow the pre-operative diet since it will help you lose weight, giving you and the surgeon greater confidence.

Reduce the chances of encountering issues. The chance of developing a medical issue before, during, or after surgery is raised when a patient is obese. Consequently, achieving a healthy weight may lessen the likelihood of this happening.

Get in the habit of doing things the correct way. When you are done with surgery, you will already know how to take care of your body by eating properly and exercising regularly.

These are the three most significant benefits of adhering to the appropriate pre-operative diet.

You must carry out each step correctly to arrive at your operation in the greatest possible condition.

Step 1: Before to beginning the actual surgical operation

At this point, the primary objective should be to cut down on calories while simultaneously increasing the intake of nutritious and low-calorie meals.

The plan is to reduce your weight to make the procedure less risky.

You have four options to choose from to complete this goal:

- Cut down on the carbs. Foods that are heavy in carbohydrates are often also high in calories. Because of this, you need to cut down on your consumption.

- In addition, following a diet reduced in carbohydrates can assist you in more efficiently maintaining stable blood sugar levels.

- Eat the appropriate kinds of proteins. Proteins assist in maintaining the structure of your muscles and give your body energy. Therefore, make it a goal to consume at least sixty grams' worth of protein daily.

- Include nutritious fats in your diet. Omega-3 fatty acids and other beneficial fats are strong buddies of your heart. In addition to lowering inflammation, they assist in the reduction of "bad" cholesterol and may shield the body against the development of cardiovascular disease.

- Be sure to stay hydrated. To keep from being dehydrated, make it a habit to consume at least one and a half liters, or half a gallon, of water each day.

At this point in your diet, you have the option of including items such as:

- Lean cuts of beef
- Breast meat from chicken or turkey
- Portions of beef or pig that are low in Fat
- Fish. For example, fish, sea bream, or salmon
- Green veggies like spinach and salad are examples.
- Vegetables like broccoli, tomatoes, or peppers
- Good fats like extra virgin olive oil
- Fruit that has just been picked, such as strawberries, peaches, and oranges.

In the meanwhile, you should steer clear of these foods:

- Platters of fast food
- Meals in a package
- The fatty cuts of beef
- Processed meats like sausages

- Deep-fried foods
- refined carbs and types of pasta
- Cheese with a high-fat content
- Alcohol
- Sugary drinks
- Sweets

In conclusion, these dietary guidelines should be adhered to for at least three weeks before the surgical procedure. Before making any changes to your diet, it is important to confirm with your primary care physician that these adjustments are appropriate for you.

Let's go to the next stage at this point.

Step 2: Two weeks before surgery

At this point, the advice from the previous week is still relevant and should be followed.

However, depending on the circumstances and the fact that you could have been taking nutritional supplements to help support you, your doctor might recommend that you cease taking certain supplements.

Therefore, you should inquire explicitly with your physician about vitamins.

Step 3: One week before surgery

Your physician may advise you to discontinue some drugs at this time.

The objective is to lessen the chance of bleeding or experiencing any other postoperative complications.

Once again, your doctor will give you instructions unique to your condition and circumstances.

Step 4: Two days before surgery

At this time, your physician may recommend that you exclude solid meals from your diet.

The previous recommendations should still be followed; therefore:

No sodas or other sugary drinks.

No alcohol

Not even coffee.

Instead of solid food, the physician will almost certainly recommend that you consume clear liquids such as broth, water, and protein shakes.

Step 5: The evening before the operation.

To be ready for the operation, you will normally be required to abstain from consuming any liquid meals or drinks.

You need to have nothing in your digestive system on the day of the procedure.

This is because, in addition to making the treatment safer, it will minimize the likelihood of difficulties arising after the operation.

Always be sure to consider your physician's recommendations. I am only walking you through the regular procedures to ensure you know what can occur.

When it comes to getting ready for bariatric surgery, these are the five steps that your physician will most likely recommend that you do.

1.3 Stages of the postoperative diet

So far, we've covered how to organize your diet before surgery.

Now that the operation is over, the following will instruct you on properly caring for your body in the postoperative period. This will offer you step-by-step instructions on how to plan out your diet weekly, as well as a list of items that should be included in your diet and foods that you should steer clear of.

In this instance, the plan will include six different stages.

It would help if you kept in mind that they are only some basic guidelines.

Your physician will provide detailed instructions about the best way to structure your healing process based on the specifics of your case.

Having stated that, let's get started with the very first step.

Step 1: 2 Days after surgery

This might be the most sensitive part of the process. Because your physical health is only starting to improve after the surgery, you need to exercise extreme caution.

In this case, limit your consumption to clear liquids, such as water, at room temperature.

Keep in mind that you should avoid drinking any drinks that are sweet, carbonated, or contain caffeine.

Step 2: Three to seven days after the surgical procedure

After the first few days, your physician may recommend consuming liquid meals instead of solid ones.

These might include:

- Fat-free Milk
- Soy drinks
- Broth

But before you do anything, you should talk to your primary care physician.

Step 3: The second week after the operation

After the first week, you'll be able to gradually include meals that are more liquid, softer, and simpler to digest into your diet.

It would help if you ate in a manner that is exceedingly slow and under control. This is the single most crucial piece of advice I can give you.

Try giving each mouthful of food around 20 chews, waiting for a moment between bits, and starting with a smaller quantity at each meal.

At this point, some permissible foods include the following; however, you should consult with your physician first:

- Protein shakes
- Creamed rice
- Yogurts without added Fat, as well as Greek yogurt
- Soups
- Fruit purée
- Ice cream or pudding that does not include any sugar

The refrain of everything and everything that wasn't on the preceding list, but in particular:

- Carbonated Drinks

- Solid foods
- Caffeine
- Sugary drinks

Step 4: Fourth step: Third week after the operation

You are now in a position to begin reintroducing solid meals. However, they should be of the sort that is soft and simple to digest.

Always remember to eat only moderate quantities at each meal and chew each mouthful a minimum of twenty times.

Salt and spices are two foods that should be avoided at all costs since they have the potential to aggravate stomach and digestive system irritation.

The following are some examples of potential novel dishes to offer:

- Eggs
- Beans
- Fish
- Lean ground beef or pork
- Cooked veggies
- Soft fruits
- Cottage cheese

However, it would be best if you continued to steer clear of any other meals.

It would help if you also kept up your healthy routines, which should include the following:

- Consume no more than three primary meals each day.
- Restrict yourself to no more than two snacks every day.
- Steer clear of greasy meals.
- Steer clear of processed meals.
- At least sixty grams of protein should be consumed each day.
- Steer clear of meals high in fiber, such as broccoli and asparagus.

- Avoid sugars
- Follow your physician's instructions on using any vitamins, minerals, or other supplements.

Now, let's go to the following stage in the process.

Step 5: The first month after the operation

It has been exactly one month since the operation was performed on you. Your body will start to recuperate and establish a new equilibrium as you eat well.

Because of this, you may also introduce solid meals and foods with a higher level of complexity.

You may now include the following to your diet:

- Sweet Potatoes
- Chicken that has been cooked to perfection.
- Cereals that do not include sugar
- Reduced-fat cheese
- Fruit.

For the time being, you should stay away from more complicated meals high in carbs or fats.

The following are some instances that should be avoided:

- Rice
- Pasta
- Bread
- Steak
- The meat that has been processed.
- Baked goodies
- Sweets
- Fibrous veggies
- Nuts

You are now prepared to go to the final stage of the process.

Step 6: Beginning in the fifth week following surgery and continuing forward

Your body will have re-established its equilibrium by this point in time.

As a result, you should feel comfortable returning to more of your regular diet.

On the other hand, you need to be very cautious about avoiding specific groups of foods, including the following:

- Quick meals
- Meat that has been processed, such as sausages
- Pommes Frites
- Deep-fried foods
- Sweets
- Fatty foods and beverages
- Drinks with Carbonation
- Sugary drinks
- Items that are made with whole milk

As a general guideline, you should avoid meals with "empty" calories.

Your stomach will be able to hold around 20% less food than it could previously; thus, you must concentrate on eating a diet high in vital elements like vitamins and minerals.

It would help if you began by reintroducing one new meal at a time so that you can monitor how your body responds to each one.

Remember to consume around 2 liters or half a gallon of water daily.

Caffeine may also be reintroduced, albeit it should be done so with caution.

Continue to lead a healthy lifestyle and if your doctor gives you the go-light, think about engaging in some physical exercise for at least thirty minutes five days a week.

From this point on, if you continue to adhere to the appropriate diet and lead a healthy lifestyle, you will continue to lose weight consistently.

1.4 Advice and Recommendations

The following is a list of some basic rules and ideas that might assist you in having success while following your gastric sleeve diet:

Avoid nonsteroidal anti-inflammatory drugs (NSAIDs) such as aspirin, naproxen, and ibuprofen. These types of over-the-counter pain medications have the potential to reduce the natural protective layer that is found on your stomach.

Make more movement a part of your life. Walking should be your first kind of exercise; if you like it, you should explore other forms of exercise, such as yoga, dance, and swimming.

The reason for this is that inactivity contributes to a sluggish metabolism, which in turn raises the likelihood of regaining lost weight.

Talk to your primary care physician about the supplements and vitamins you're considering taking so that they can guide you in making the best decision.

Consuming alcohol and food at the same time is not recommended.

To avoid being dehydrated, you should maintain drinking water or electrolyte drinks that are low in calories throughout the day.

Steer clear of meals that are highly processed, fried, and high in trans fats.

Avoid foods that are high in concentrated sugars.

Avoid eating foods that are high in calories but low in nutrients.

Chew slowly when you eat.

It is important not to overeat since your stomach will become bigger and then return to its normal size.

Learn to distinguish between the hunger caused by your body and the hunger caused by your emotions or mental state.

When preparing your meals, you must use a blender or food processor.

Chapter 2 Early Post-Operative Diet

2.1 Soymilk Shake

Preparation time- 5 minutes | Cook time- 0 minutes | Servings- 4

Nutritional value- Calories- 144 | Fat- 0g | Protein- 14g | Carbohydrates- 21g

Ingredients:

- 4 Cups soy milk
- 1 cup soy milk powder or fat-free dry milk powder

Instructions:

- Put the soy milk and the milk powder in a blender and mix them. Blend on high for five minutes until the powder is completely dissolved and can no longer be seen.
- Put any milk leftover into a container that can seal tightly to keep the freshness in. The taste will become better with time.
- Discard any remaining milk after 7 days.

2.2 Mango Pineapple Shake

Preparation time- 5 minutes | Cook time- 0 minutes | Servings- 2

Nutritional value- Calories- 114 | Fat- 2.5g | Protein- 15g | Carbohydrates- 9g

Ingredients:

1 cup unsweetened soy milk or fat-free milk

1/4 cup (1 scoop) vanilla protein powder

¼ cup mango chunks, frozen

¼ cup pineapple chunks or canned, drained

1/2 cup low-fat plain yogurt

5 ice cubes

Instructions:

Put the unsweetened soy milk, the vanilla protein powder, the mango chunks, the pineapple chunks, the plain yogurt, and the ice cubes into a blender. Blend until smooth.

Blend for around three to four minutes until the protein powder is completely dissolved and cannot be seen.

After separating the shake into two glasses, you may then enjoy it.

Any extra shake should be stored in the refrigerator in a container to keep air out for up to a week. Re-mix before serving.

2.3 Soupy Chicken

Preparation time- 10 minutes | Cook time- 6 hours | Servings- 8

Nutritional value- Calories- 120 | Fat- 0g | Protein- 16g | Carbohydrates- 8g

Ingredients:

- 3 lb. bone-in chicken breasts
- 5 medium carrots, chopped into chunks
- 4 celery stalks, chopped into chunks
- medium yellow onion, cut into chunks
- 1 tbsp organic apple cider vinegar
- 1 tbsp Himalayan pink salt, fine (optional)

- 3 bay leaves
- 1/2 tsp black pepper, ground
- 10 cups water, enough to cover
- 8 scoops plain protein powder, divided per serving

Instructions:

- Place chicken breasts with bones still in them, carrot pieces, celery chunks, onion chunks, apple cider vinegar, fine Himalayan pink salt (if using), bay leaves, and freshly ground black pepper in the bottom of a slow cooker. Cover with enough water to completely submerge the ingredients.
- Cover the slow cooker and cook on high heat for a total of six hours or on low heat for a total of twelve hours.
- After the chicken broth has finished cooking, separate the chicken flesh from the bones and place both the bones and the chicken meat in separate airtight containers to be frozen for later use in other dishes.
- After allowing the chicken broth to reach room temperature, filter the solids out of it. Throw away all of the solids.
- Each of the 8 airtight containers should have 1 cup of chicken broth poured into it, and the containers should be sealed.
- The chicken broth may be kept in the refrigerator for up to seven days. You may keep any leftover broth in the freezer for up to six months.
- When ready to serve, simmer the cold chicken broth over low heat until it is warm but not boiling. Stir in one level scoop of plain protein powder, and then serve.

2.4 Chicken Squash

Preparation time- 5 minutes | Cook time- 15 minutes | Servings- 4

Nutritional value- Calories- 71 | Fat- 4g | Protein- 2g | Carbohydrates- 9g

Ingredients:

- 1 tbsp coconut oil

- 10 oz butternut squash, cubed
- 1 ½ cups unsalted chicken broth
- Sea salt, fine
- Black pepper, ground
- Cinnamon, ground
- 2 tbsp non-fat plain yogurt, divided
- 2 tbsp parsley, finely chopped and divided

Instructions:

- Put a stockpot of medium size over high heat, add the coconut oil, butternut squash that has been diced, and unsalted chicken broth, and bring to a boil. Cook the butternut squash for ten minutes or until it reaches the desired consistency.
- Take the stockpot from the heat and empty its contents into a blender.
- The butternut squash should be puréed until it is smooth. To taste, season with finely powdered black pepper and sea salt that has been crushed finely.
- After dividing the butternut squash soup among four bowls for serving, add some ground cinnamon on top of each dish, followed by 1 and 1/2 teaspoons of non-fat plain yogurt and some finely chopped parsley, and then enjoy the soup.

2.5 Mixed Berries Shake

Preparation time- 5 minutes | Cook time- 0 minutes | Servings- 2

Nutritional value- Calories- 145 | Fat- 3g | Protein- 15g | Carbohydrates- 15g

Ingredients:

- 1 cup fat-free milk or unsweetened soy milk
- 1 cup fresh or frozen mixed berries
- 1/2 cup non-fat plain yogurt
- ¼ cup (1 scoop) plain protein powder
- ½ tsp vanilla extract

Instructions:

- Put the milk or soy milk, plain yogurt, plain protein powder, fresh or frozen mixed berries, and vanilla extract into a blender.

- Put the milk or soy milk, plain yogurt, plain protein powder, fresh or frozen mixed berries, and vanilla extract into a blender.

- Enjoy the berry shake when you pour half of it into a glass and serve it yourself.
- Put any remaining shake in the refrigerator and give it a quick whirl before serving. After a week, throw away any shake that is still left.

2.6 Vanilla Shake

Preparation time- 5 minutes | Cook time- 0 minutes | Servings- 2

Nutritional value- Calories- 153 | Fat- 3g | Protein- 22g | Carbohydrates- 8g

Ingredients:

- 1 cup soy milk or low-fat milk
- 1/2 Cup (1 scoop) vanilla protein powder
- ¼ cup low-fat plain kefir
- ½ cup low-fat plain yogurt
- 1 tsp vanilla extract
- 5 ice cubes

Instructions:

- In a blender, combine the milk or soy milk, vanilla protein powder, kefir, low-fat plain yogurt, and vanilla extract. Blend on high for three to four minutes or until all ingredients are well combined.
- Enjoy the vanilla shake once you've poured half of it into a glass.
- Any extra shake should be stored in an airtight jar in the refrigerator for up to one week. Re-blend before serving.

2.7 Choco mint Milkshake

Preparation time- 10 minutes | Cook time- 0 minutes | Servings- 2

Nutritional value- Calories- 275 | Fat- 3g | Protein- 20g | Carbohydrates- 18g

Ingredients:

- 1 cup fat-free milk or soy milk

- 1/2 cup low-fat plain cottage cheese
- ¼ cup (1 scoop) chocolate protein powder
- 1 tbsp unsweetened cocoa powder
- 2 tbsp mint leaves
- 4 ice cubes

Instructions:

- Put the fat-free milk or the soy milk, the plain cottage cheese, the chocolate protein powder, the unsweetened cocoa powder, the mint leaves, and the ice into a blender. Blend until smooth.
- Combine until there are no lumps.
- Enjoy the mint shake by dividing it in half and pouring it into two glasses.
- You may keep any leftover milkshake in an airtight jar in the refrigerator for up to a week. Before serving, please give it a quick whirl in the blender.

2.8 Pea Pottage

Preparation time- 5 minutes | Cook time- 20 minutes | Servings- 5

Nutritional value- Calories- 116 | Fat- 4g | Protein- 11g | Carbohydrates- 9g

Ingredients:

- 1 tbsp olive oil
- 1 (10 oz) frozen peas
- 4 oz bacon, cut into small cubes
- 1 ½ cups low-sodium chicken or vegetable broth
- 1/3 cup non-fat plain yogurt
- Black pepper, ground
- ¼ cup parsley, chopped for garnish

Instructions:

- Heat the olive oil in a medium stockpot over medium-high heat until hot.

- Bring the frozen peas, bacon cubes, and low-sodium chicken or veggie broth to a boil. Cook, occasionally stirring, for 10 minutes or until the peas soften.

- Turn off the heat in the stockpot.

- Puree the soup in a blender until it is smooth. Divide the soup into 5 bowls, top with 1 tablespoon of plain yogurt, and season with ground black pepper to taste.

- Serve garnished with parsley, and enjoy.

2.9 Creamy Carrot Soup

Preparation time- 10 minutes | Cook time- 30 minutes | Servings- 4

Nutritional value- Calories- 44 | Fat- 2g | Protein- 4g | Carbohydrates- 3g

Ingredients:

- 1 cup carrots, peeled and sliced
- 2 tsp stevia extract
- ½ tbsp olive oil
- Sea salt, fine
- ¾ Cup non-fat plain yogurt
- ¼ Cup unsweetened almond milk

Instructions:

- Preheat the oven to 425°F/gas mark 7 and set aside. Set aside a baking tray covered with aluminum foil.

- Mix the sliced carrots, stevia extract, and olive oil in a medium-sized dish until evenly coated.

- Sprinkle fine sea salt over the carrot slices in the preheated baking pan.

- Bake for 25 to 30 minutes or until softened and beginning to caramelize.

- Combine the cooked carrots, plain yogurt, and unsweetened almond milk in a blender.

- Blend for 1 minute or until the mixture becomes a puree. Serve immediately and enjoy.

- Refrigerate any leftover carrot puree in an airtight jar for up to 5 days.

2.10 Hearty Tomato

Preparation time- 10 minutes | Cook time- 30 minutes | Servings- 4

Nutritional value- Calories- 121 | Fat- 7g | Protein- 4g | Carbohydrates- 9g

Ingredients:

- 2 tbsp olive oil
- ¼ cup red onion, diced
- 1 (15 oz) can low sodium diced tomatoes in juice
- 8 oz unsalted vegetable stock
- 1 tsp basil, finely chopped
- 2 tsp stevia extract
- 1 tsp balsamic vinegar (optional)
- Sea salt, fine
- Black pepper, ground
- 8 tbsp low-fat plain yogurt

Instructions:

- In a medium-sized stockpot, heat the olive oil over medium heat. Add the onion and cook for 5 minutes or until it has softened.

- Bring the soup to a boil after adding the diced tomatoes with their juices, vegetable broth without salt, and chopped basil. Allow the soup to boil on low heat for 10 to 15 minutes.

- Take away from the heat.

- Blend the tomato soup in a blender until completely smooth.

- Add the extract of stevia and the balsamic vinegar (if using). Mix fine sea salt and freshly ground black pepper into the soup.

- Pour the soup into four dishes and top each with 2 tablespoons of plain yogurt before serving.

2.11 Double Fudge Chocolate Shake

Preparation time- 5 minutes | Cook time- 0 minutes | Servings- 2

Nutritional value- Calories- 157 | Fat- 1g | Protein- 20g | Carbohydrates- 18g

Ingredients:

- 1 cup low-fat milk or unsweetened soy milk
- ½ cup low-fat plain Greek yogurt
- 1 scoop (¼ cup) chocolate protein powder
- 2 tablespoons unsweetened cocoa powder
- ½ small banana
- ½ tsp. vanilla extract

Instructions:

- Put the milk, yogurt, protein powder, cocoa powder, banana, and vanilla extract into a blender. Blend on high speed for two to three minutes or until the drink is completely smooth and the powders have been dissolved.

- Enjoy the shake by transferring half of it to a glass.

- Any shake that is not consumed or used immediately should be stored in the refrigerator in an airtight container for up to one week. Mix it up again just before you serve it.

2.12 Peanut Butter Cup Shake

Preparation time- 5 minutes | Cook time- 0 minutes | Servings- 2

Nutritional value- Calories- 215 | Fat- 3g | Protein- 27g | Carbohydrates- 18g

Ingredients:

- 1 cup of low-fat milk
- ½ cup low-fat plain Greek yogurt
- ¼ cup non-fat ricotta cheese
- 1 scoop (¼ cup) chocolate protein powder
- 2 tbsps. powdered peanut butter
- 2 tbsps. cocoa powder

Instructions:

- Put the milk, yogurt, and ricotta in a blender. Add the protein powder, powdered peanut butter, and chocolate powder. Blend until smooth. Blend on high for three to four minutes until the granules are completely dissolved and no longer visible, whichever comes first.
- Enjoy the shake by transferring half of it to a glass.
- Any shake that is not consumed or used immediately should be stored in the refrigerator in an airtight container for up to one week. Mix it up again just before you serve it.

2.13 Mango Smoothie

Preparation time- 10 minutes | Cook time- 0 minutes | Servings- 2

Nutritional value- Calories- 115 | Fat- 3g | Protein- 15g | Carbohydrates- 9g

Ingredients:

- 1 cup unsweetened coconut milk or low-fat milk
- 1 scoop (¼ cup) vanilla protein powder
- ¼ cup frozen mango chunks

- ¼ cup canned pineapple chunks in 100% natural juice or water, drained
- ½ cup low-fat plain Greek yogurt
- 5 ice cubes

Instructions:

- Put the milk, protein powder, mango, and pineapple chunks, as well as the yogurt, into a blender. Blend until smooth. Blend at high speed for three to four minutes or until the powder is completely dissolved and cannot be seen anymore.
- Enjoy a glass of the smoothie once you've poured half of it into the glass.
- Any shake that is not consumed or used immediately should be stored in the refrigerator in an airtight container for up to one week. Mix it up again just before you serve it.

2.14 Classic Tuna Salad

Preparation time- 10 minutes | Cook time- 0 minutes | Servings- 3

Nutritional value- Calories- 73 | Fat- 2g | Protein- 11g | Carbohydrates- 3g

Ingredients:

- 1 (5-ounce) can of water-packed tuna
- 1 tbsp freshly squeezed lemon juice
- 1 tbsp olive oil-based mayonnaise
- 1 tbsp low-fat plain Greek yogurt
- ½ tsp Dijon mustard
- 1 tbsp finely chopped red onion
- 1 tsp pickle relish or finely chopped pickles
- ½ tsp freshly ground black pepper

Instructions:

- Drain the tuna over the sink using a sieve with a very fine mesh. It should be transferred to a small bowl.
- Mix the tuna with the lemon juice, mayonnaise, Greek yogurt, Dijon mustard, red onion, pickle relish, and ground black pepper until evenly distributed throughout the tuna.
- If you want to enhance the taste, serve it straight away, cover it, or chill it overnight.

2.15 Chicken Salad

Preparation time- 10 minutes | Cook time- 10 minutes | Servings- 7

Nutritional value- Calories- 84 | Fat- 2g | Protein- 16g | Carbohydrates- 1g

Ingredients:

2 tbsps low-fat plain Greek yogurt

1 tbsp olive oil-based mayonnaise

1 tbsp freshly squeezed lemon juice

1 tsp curry powder

1½ cups diced cooked chicken or 1 (12.5-ounce) can chicken breast

Instructions:

- Blend the yogurt, mayonnaise, lemon juice, and curry powder in a bowl of medium size until the ingredients are well blended.

- Add the chicken to the bowl, then mix everything until everything is incorporated and the chicken is completely covered in the coating.

- If you want to enhance the taste, serve it straight away, cover it, or chill it overnight.

2.16 Fried Beans

Preparation time- 10 minutes | Cook time- 5 minutes | Servings- 4

Nutritional value- Calories- 121 | Fat- 1g | Protein- 7g | Carbohydrates- 20g

Ingredients:

1 tsp extra-virgin olive oil

1 tsp minced garlic

1 (15-ounce) can of black beans, drained and rinsed

1 tbsp freshly squeezed lime juice

1 tsp smoked paprika

½ tsp dried oregano

¼ tsp cayenne pepper

½ tsp ground cumin

Instructions:

- Warm the olive oil in a small saucepan set over medium-low heat, then add the garlic to the pan. Stir for 1 minute. After adding the beans, continue to simmer for about 5 minutes or until they are heated throughout. Remove the pot from the heat. Mix the ingredients well after adding the lime juice, paprika, oregano, cayenne, and cumin.

- The beans may be mashed with a potato masher, pureed using a blender or immersion blender, or pureed using either method to get the appropriate consistency.

- Serve and enjoy

2.17 Superfood Smoothie

Preparation time- 5 minutes | Cook time- 0 minutes | Servings- 2

Nutritional value- Calories- 148 | Fat- 4g | Protein- 13g | Carbohydrates- 18g

Ingredients:

- 1 cup fresh spinach
- 1 kiwi fruit, peeled and cut into chunks
- ½ medium cucumber, peeled
- ½ small banana
- 1 cup unsweetened almond milk or low-fat milk
- 1 tbsp ground flaxseed
- 1 tsp chia seeds
- 1 scoop (¼ cup) unflavored or vanilla protein powder
- 10 to 12 ice cubes

Instructions:

- Put the spinach, kiwi, cucumber, banana, milk, flaxseed, chia seeds, and protein powder into a blender. Blend until smooth. Serve immediately. Blend the ingredients at high speed for two to three minutes until the smoothie is completely lump-free and smooth. If the shake is too thick for your liking, add anywhere from two to four tablespoons of water and blend it all.

- Enjoy the shake by transferring half of it to a glass.

- Any shake that is not consumed or used immediately should be stored in the refrigerator in an airtight container for up to one week. Mix well just before serving.

2.18 Apple Pie Shake

Preparation time- 5 minutes | Cook time- 0 minutes | Servings- 2

Nutritional value- Calories- 123 | Fat- 1g | Protein- 14g | Carbohydrates- 14g

Ingredients:

- 1 cup of low-fat milk
- 1 scoop (¼ cup) vanilla protein powder
- 1 small apple, peeled, cored, and chopped
- 1 tsp vanilla extract
- 2 tsps ground cinnamon
- ½ tsp ground nutmeg
- 5 ice cubes

Instructions:

- Put the milk, protein powder, apple, vanilla, cinnamon, and nutmeg into a blender. Blend until smooth. Add the ice cubes. Blend at high speed for three to four minutes or until the powder is completely dissolved and cannot be seen anymore.
- Enjoy the shake by transferring half of it to a glass.
- Any shake that is not consumed or used immediately should be stored in the refrigerator in an airtight container for up to one week. Mix it up again just before you serve it.

2.19 Super Soup

Preparation time- 5 minutes | Cook time- 15 minutes | Servings- 4

Nutritional value- Calories- 32 | Fat- 1g | Protein- 1g | Carbohydrates- 3g

Ingredients:

- 2 sliced spring onions to serve
- Nori seaweed to serve
- 2 tbsps. of Nutra Organics Collagen Powder

- 2 tbsps. of wheat-free tamari soy sauce
- 2 tbsps. of Shiro miso paste
- 3 garlic cloves, smashed
- Small 10g ginger knob, finely sliced
- 4 cups of filtered water

Instructions:

- Bring the water to a rolling boil in a big saucepan made of stainless steel.
- After the heat has been reduced, add the ginger that has been sliced and then let the mixture simmer for around ten minutes. Put an end to the heat.
- Mix the miso paste, tamari, and collagen powder until well combined.
- Try it out, then make any necessary adjustments to the garlic and ginger. Just before serving, fold the onions in so they are evenly distributed.
- Place the soup in dishes and top with nori seaweed before serving.

2.20 Creamy Smoothie

Preparation time- 5 minutes | Cook time- 0 minutes | Servings- 2

Nutritional value- Calories- 275 | Fat- 11g | Protein- 15g | Carbohydrates- 22g

Ingredients:

- 1/4 cup of fresh carrot juice (optional)
- Dash of ground clove and cardamom (optional plus spice)
- Dash of ground nutmeg
- Dash of black pepper
- Dash of ground cinnamon
- 1 tbsp of fresh ginger (plus more to taste)
- 1/2 tsp of ground turmeric powder
- 1 cup of light coconut or almond milk (Best use full-fat coconut)

- 1 cup of the frozen ripe banana (sliced)

Instructions:

- In a powerful blender, combine the coconut milk, banana, cinnamon, turmeric, black pepper, nutmeg, and ginger.

- Blend on high speed until the mixture is completely smooth and creamy. Mix freshly squeezed carrot juice, cardamom, and clove (if used).

- If the smoothie is too thin, add frozen banana; if it is too thick, add more water or coconut milk.

- Taste and adjust taste as desired. (Add black pepper for a spicy flavor, ginger for a zing, cinnamon for warming, banana and carrot juice for sweetness and color, and turmeric for an earthy undertone.)

- Serve, and enjoy!

Chapter 3 Breakfast Recipes

3.1 Blueberry Pancakes

Preparation time- 5 minutes | Cook time- 5 minutes | Servings- 2

Nutritional value- Calories- 358 | Fat- 11g | Protein- 27g | Carbohydrates- 34g

Ingredients:

- 1 cup blueberries
- 3 eggs
- 1 1/2 tbsp. coconut oil, melted
- 1/2 cup whole wheat flour
- 2 tbsp. vanilla protein powder
- Non-stick spray for cooking

Instructions:

- In a bowl, thoroughly combine the eggs.
- Ensure the wheat flour, vanilla protein powder, blueberries, and coconut oil are well combined before adding the wheat flour.
- Next, spray non-stick spray.
- Add part of the batter, and then continue to cook until the color changes to a light brown on each side.
- Your pancakes are now ready to be served when they are done cooking.

3.2 Peach Smoothie

Preparation time- 13 minutes | Cook time- 0 minutes | Servings- 2

Nutritional value- Calories- 281 | Fat- 12g | Protein- 16g | Carbohydrates- 28g

Ingredients:

- 1 cup peaches, frozen
- 1 cup of non-fat milk
- 1 cup vanilla Greek yogurt
- 1 avocado, peeled and pitted
- 1 tbsp. flaxseed, ground
- 1 tsp stevia, granulated
- 1 tsp pure vanilla extract
- 1-2 cups ice cubes

Instructions:

- Place all of the ingredients in a blender and mix until smooth. Purée until smooth.
- Serve quickly.

3.3 Chicken Tart

Preparation time- 10 minutes | Cook time- 40 minutes | Servings- 8

Nutritional value- Calories- 186 | Fat- 10g | Protein- 20g | Carbohydrates- 4g

Ingredients:

- Cooking spray
- 1 ¼ cups (6 oz.) chicken breast, cooked and cubed
- 4 oz. sharp cheddar cheese, shredded or cubed
- 8 oz. mozzarella cheese, shredded
- ½ tsp basil, finely chopped
- ½ tsp oregano, finely chopped
- ½ tsp thyme, finely chopped
- ½ tsp chives, finely chopped
- 3 large eggs
- 1 cup of non-fat milk

Instructions:

- Prepare the oven by preheating it to 400 degrees Fahrenheit and marking it with a 6.
- Spray a pie dish with cooking spray and set aside.
- In a pie pan, layer the chicken cut up into cubes, shredded cheddar cheese, and mozzarella cheese.
- The chopped basil, oregano, thyme, and chopped chives should all be sprinkled on top.
- In a dish of about medium size, whisk together the big eggs and the non-fat milk.
- After the chicken and cheese have been coated, pour the egg mixture on top.
- Bake for forty minutes or until the top begins to brown.
- The tart should rest for 5 minutes before being served shortly after.

- Keep the savory tart in the refrigerator for up to a week. Warm it up again before you serve it.

3.4 Apple Avocado Juice

Preparation time- 10 minutes | Cook time- 0 minutes | Servings- 2

Nutritional value- Calories- 275 | Fat- 3g | Protein- 20g | Carbohydrates- 18g

Ingredients:

- 2 baby carrots
- 1 little avocado
- 2 little apples
- 2 tbsp. of lemon juice

Instructions:

- Squeeze a lemon to get the required amount of juice. Get the juice out of it by straining it.
- After peeling them with a potato peeler, wash the baby carrots and chop them into bite-sized pieces.
- Remove the core, hard pieces, and seeds from both apples before cleaning them. Split them up into little bits.
- Use the other half of the avocado in the same way.
- Fill your juicer or extractor with carrots, lemon juice, avocado, and apple chunks.
- Scoop the juice from the fruit into a dish.
- Blend the ingredients by stirring.
- Now serve in two glasses with ice cubes and the juice of one avocado, one apple, and one lemon.

3.5 Scrambler Egg

Preparation time- 5 minutes | Cook time- 15 minutes | Servings- 4

Nutritional value- Calories- 150 | Fat- 10g | Protein- 12g | Carbohydrates- 3g

Ingredients:

- 1/4 cup of 2% shredded cheddar cheese
- 4 strips of turkey bacon
- 1/2 cup of chopped red bell pepper
- 5 eggs
- 3/4 cup of cherry tomatoes

Instructions:

- Cook the turkey bacon over medium heat, flipping once until it is brown and crispy on both sides.
- Set the turkey bacon aside to cool on a cutting board.
- Toss the bell pepper and cherry tomatoes in a skillet and cook over medium heat, stirring occasionally. As that is happening, chop up some turkey bacon.
- When the cherry tomatoes start to "blister," whip the eggs with a fork and throw them in the pan. With a fork, continually whisk the eggs and other ingredients to scramble them.
- Blend the turkey bacon and cheese.
- Quickly dish it out.

3.6 Pumpkin Latte

Preparation time- 10 minutes | Cook time- 5 minutes | Servings- 1

Nutritional value- Calories- 202 | Fat- 5g | Protein- 25g | Carbohydrates- 13g

Ingredients:

- 2 almond milk creamer
- Cinnamon for garnishing
- 1 scoop of vanilla protein powder
- 8 oz. of freshly brewed coffee
- Whip cream for garnishing
- 1 oz. of pumpkin puree

Instructions:

Prepare coffee.

In a cup, combine the creamer, protein, and pumpkin until the mixture resembles pudding. Continue whisking until no lumps remain.

Then, carefully pour in the coffee while continuously stirring the mixture.

Add a sprinkle of cinnamon and a dollop of whipped cream for garnish.

3.7 Radish Hash

Preparation time- 5 minutes | Cook time- 15 minutes | Servings- 4

Nutritional value- Calories- 211 | Fat- 12g | Protein- 11g | Carbohydrates- 4g

Ingredients:

- 4 eggs
- 1 lb. of radishes
- Olive oil
- 8 oz. of turkey sausage
- 1/2 onion
- 1 teaspoon of minced garlic
- Salt and pepper

Instructions:

- Small cubes of onion and radishes should be prepared.
- Combine the radishes, salt, onions, garlic, and pepper in a hot skillet with olive oil.
- Cook them until they are soft and golden. Cook the turkey sausage until it is finished.
- Take the hash out of the pan, then scramble the eggs to your liking. Serve the hash with the egg on top.

3.8 Chicken Pineapple Skewers

Preparation time- 5 minutes | Cook time- 10 minutes | Servings- 4

Nutritional value- Calories- 101 | Fat- 3g | Protein- 13g | Carbohydrates- 6g

Ingredients:

- 4 links of chicken sausage pre-cooked
- 1 cup of fresh pineapple chunks

Instructions:

- Preheat a grill to medium-high heat.

- Cut the links of chicken sausage into 1-inch chunks. If you have not previously done so, slice the pineapple.

- On skewers, thread two chicken sausages, each pineapple chunk.

- Each side should be grilled for about four minutes. Remove the skewers from the grill and serve them as soon as possible.

- A low-sugar barbecue sauce may also be sprayed on the skewers before grilling.

3.9 Bacon Eggy Bites

Preparation time- 5 minutes | Cook time- 25 minutes | Servings- 12

Nutritional value- Calories- 110 | Fat- 8g | Protein- 9g | Carbohydrates- 0g

Ingredients:

- 8 slices of cooked bacon
- Salt and black pepper
- 2 teaspoons of sour cream
- 1 cup of grated gruyere cheese
- 10 eggs

Instructions:

- Whisk together the eggs, cheese, salt, sour cream, and pepper in a large bowl.

- Whisk the eggs until they are light and airy to make them airy.

- Reserve a muffin tin coated with cooking spray

- Set the oven temperature to 300 degrees Fahrenheit.

- Separate each bacon slice into three smaller pieces. Create an X in each egg cup using two pieces.

- Bake the egg cups until they are hard (it will take around 25 minutes).

3.10 Greek Omelet

Preparation time- 5 minutes | Cook time- 10 minutes | Servings- 2

Nutritional value- Calories- 154 | Fat- 7g | Protein- 15g | Carbohydrates- 9g

Ingredients:

- 1/4 cup of feta cheese low-fat
- 2 tablespoons of chopped red onion
- 1/4 cup of 2% cottage cheese
- 2 eggs
- 1/2 cup of spinach leaves
- 2 tablespoons of seeded, chopped tomatoes
- 1/2 tablespoon of chopped garlic

Instructions:

- Cook the spinach, onions, and garlic over the medium temperature in a small non-stick skillet. Stir continuously, and when the onions become soft, add the tomatoes.
- Eggs and cottage cheese are combined in a mixing basin. Turn the spinach mixture to evenly coat the pan.
- Cook for about two to three minutes, covered, or until the eggs are almost set.
- Continue cooking for an additional minute after adding 3 tablespoons of cheese. Slide a spatula underneath the omelet and fold it in half to remove it.
- Remove the skillet from the heat and cut it in half.
- Serve and enjoy.

3.11 Zucchini Hash

Preparation time- 5 minutes | Cook time- 15 minutes | Servings- 4

Nutritional value- Calories- 106 | Fat- 6g | Protein- 12g | Carbohydrates- 6g

Ingredients:

- 8 oz. of sliced mushrooms
- 1 onion large
- 4 eggs
- 6 slices of diced turkey bacon
- 2 zucchinis diced
- 2 cups of baby spinach
- Salt and pepper, to taste

Instructions:

- Prepare the onions and zucchini by slicing them very thinly.
- Put a sprinkle of olive oil in a hot pan and then preheat it.
- After it is browned, take the turkey bacon out of the pan.
- Once all the veggies have been added, please give them a brief sauté over a high temperature.
- Prepare the egg nine according to your tastes.
- If you so want, garnish with some fresh herbs.

3.12 Classic Enchiladas

Preparation time- 5 minutes | Cook time- 20 minutes | Servings- 8

Nutritional value- Calories- 197 | Fat- 14g | Protein- 22g | Carbohydrates- 3g

Ingredients:

- 1 onion diced
- 1/2 cup of shredded cheddar

- 1 lb. of turkey sausage
- 1/2 cup of salsa
- 8 eggs
- 2 sour cream
- 1 bell pepper diced

Instructions:

- Beat eggs and cook them in a pan as if making an omelet, but don't fill them. Arrange them on a dish.
- Cook the sausage, onions, and peppers together.
- After filling each egg with 1/8 of the sausage mixture, roll them up.
- Please place them in a baking dish and sprinkle salsa and cheese.
- Preheat the oven to 350 degrees Fahrenheit and bake for 12 minutes.
- Serve topped with a spoonful of sour cream.

3.13 Fruits Oat

Preparation time- 10 minutes | Cook time- 45 minutes | Servings- 6

Nutritional value- Calories- 149 | Fat- 4g | Protein- 8g | Carbohydrates- 21g

Ingredients:

- Cooking spray
- 1 cup rolled oats
- 1/2 tsp cinnamon, ground
- 3/4 tsp baking powder
- 1 tbsp. chia seeds, ground
- 3 large eggs
- 1 cup soy milk
- 1/2 cup low-fat plain yogurt,

- 1 tsp vanilla extract
- 1 tsp liquid stevia (optional)
- 1 cup mixed nuts, roughly chopped
- 1 cup mixed dried fruit, roughly chopped

Instructions:

- Preheat the oven to 375 degrees Fahrenheit and gas mark 5. Prepare a deep baking dish and put it aside after being sprayed with cooking spray.

- In a dish suitable for mixing, combine the rolled oats, the powdered cinnamon, the baking powder, and the ground chia seeds.

- In a second large mixing bowl, whisk together the big eggs, soy milk, plain yogurt, vanilla extract, and liquid stevia (if using). Continue whisking until all of the ingredients are mixed.

- Mix the oat mixture with the egg mixture, thoroughly blending the two before serving.

- Mix in the roughly chopped mixed nuts as well as the coarsely chopped mixed dried fruit.

- Put the baking dish into the oven and bake for about 45 minutes, or until the edges of the dish begin to separate from the pan's sides. When touched, the oatmeal will softly spring back into its original shape.

- Enjoy the oat bake by dividing it up between six individual serving dishes.

- You may save any leftover oat bake by placing it in a container with an airtight glass bottom and refrigerating it for up to a week for a quick and simple breakfast. Alternatively, you can freeze it in an airtight plastic container.

3.14 Savory Soufflé

Preparation time- 5 minutes | Cook time- 15 minutes | Servings- 1

Nutritional value- Calories- 124 | Fat- 6g | Protein- 13g | Carbohydrates- 5g

Ingredients:

- 1 large free-range egg,
- 1/4 cup of non-fat milk
- Sea Salt, fine
- Black pepper, ground
- 1 oz. any cold meat, chopped
- 1/2 tomato, pulp removed and diced
- 2 tbsp. fat-free cheddar cheese, shredded
- 1 tsp chives, chopped (optional)
- 1 tsp green onion, chopped (optional)

Instructions:

- Prepare a baking temperature of 350 degrees Fahrenheit and a gas mark of 4 in the oven.

- Whisk the giant egg, non-fat milk, fine sea salt, and powdered black pepper together in a basin of medium size until the ingredients are completely incorporated. Do not over-mix.

- Mix in your preferred cold meat after adding it to the dish.

- The egg mixture should be poured into a ramekin between small and medium in size, and then the diced tomato, shredded cheddar cheese, minced chives, and chopped green onion should be sprinkled on top (if using).

- Bake for ten to fifteen minutes or until the egg has reached the desired consistency and the cheese has melted.

- Take the soufflé out of the oven, place it on a cooling rack, and wait for it to cool completely before serving. To be served hot.

3.15 Salmon Bruschetta

Preparation time- 5 minutes | Cook time- 10 minutes | Servings- 4

Nutritional value- Calories- 231 | Fat- 10g | Protein- 18g | Carbohydrates- 19g

Ingredients:

- 2 tbsp. low-fat plain yogurt
- 1/2 lemon, juiced
- 1 ripe avocado, halved and pit removed
- 4 slices whole-grain bread
- 1 garlic clove
- 8 oz smoked salmon
- 2 fresh dill sprigs

Instructions:

- Combine the plain yogurt and fresh lemon juice in a small mixing dish.

- Scoop out the avocado and mash it until no lumps remain. Mix it well with the yogurt mixture in a bowl.

- Toast the bread and rub each piece with a full garlic clove.

- Toast topped with avocado and yogurt mixture and 2 ounces of smoked salmon.

- Garnish each piece with dill.

- Serve and enjoy.

3.16 Pecan Pikelets

Preparation time- 10 minutes | Cook time- 0 minutes | Servings- 2

Nutritional value- Calories- 275 | Fat- 3g | Protein- 20g | Carbohydrates- 18g

Ingredients:

- Cooking spray
- 1 cup almond flour
- 1/2 cup unsweetened coconut milk
- 2 large free-range eggs
- 2 tsp vanilla extract
- 1 tsp cinnamon, ground
- 1 tsp baking powder
- 1/4 tsp stevia
- 1/4 tsp sea salt, fine

Instructions:

- Apply cooking spray to a skillet or crepe pan and heat over medium heat.

- Whisk together the almond flour, unsweetened coconut milk, large eggs, vanilla extract, ground cinnamon, baking powder, stevia, and fine sea salt in a medium mixing bowl.

- Add two tablespoons of batter to the pan.

- Cook for 1 to 2 minutes on each side until golden brown.
- Repeat with the remaining batter, ensuring that each pikelet is cooked separately if cooking many cakes at once.
- Remove the pikelets from the pan and serve them plain or with the topping of your choice.

3.17 Acorn Squash

Preparation time- 10 minutes | Cook time- 50 minutes | Servings- 3

Nutritional value- Calories- 424 | Fat- 21g | Protein- 20g | Carbohydrates- 18g

Ingredients:

- 1 lb. tofu, firm
- 1 tsp basil
- 1 pinch of black pepper, freshly ground
- 1 tsp onion, chopped finely
- 1 tsp garlic powder
- 1 cup cheddar cheese, reduced-fat, grated
- 2 pieces acorn squash, halved, seeded
- 1 cup celery, diced
- 1 cup mushrooms, fresh, sliced
- 1 tsp oregano
- 1/8 tsp salt
- 8 oz. tomato sauce

Instructions:

- Preheat the oven to 350 degrees Fahrenheit.
- Arrange the acorn squash pieces in the bottom of a glass dish, and cut the sides down.

- Place in the microwave for about 20 minutes or until softened.
- Place aside.
- Heat a non-stick saucepan over medium heat, then add the tofu (sliced into cubes).
- Cook until the onion and celery are cooked before adding them.
- Cook for another 2 minutes or until the onion is transparent.
- Mix in the mushrooms. Cook for another 2 to 3 minutes, stirring occasionally. Pour in the tomato sauce and season with salt and pepper.
- Stir everything together, then pour equal amounts of the mixture into the acorn squash pieces.
- Cook for about fifteen minutes, covered in the oven. Before returning to the oven, remove the lid and top with the cheese. Cook for 5 minutes or until the cheese is melted and bubbling.
- Serve right away.

3.18 Cinnamon Chiller

Preparation time- 5 minutes | Cook time- 0 minutes | Servings- 1

Nutritional value- Calories- 179 | Fat- 5g | Protein- 23g | Carbohydrates- 8g

Ingredients:
- 1 cup almond milk, unsweetened
- 2 tbsp vanilla protein powder
- 1/2 tsp cinnamon
- 1/4 tsp vanilla extract
- 1 tbsp chia seeds
- 1 cup ice cubs

Instructions:
- To make the smoothie, place all of the ingredients in a blender.
- Mix it up until it has the consistency of cream.

- Serve cold, and have fun with it!

3.19 Sweet Potato Waffles

Preparation time- 5 minutes | Cook time- 10 minutes | Servings- 2

Nutritional value- Calories- 343 | Fat- 10g | Protein- 12g | Carbohydrates- 54g

Ingredients:

- 1/2 a cup of sweet potato
- 1 cup oats
- 2 eggs
- 1 cup of almond milk
- 1 tbsp honey
- Maple syrup (based on your preference)
- 2 bananas, sliced
- 1/4 tsp baking powder
- 1 tbsp olive oil
- Cooking spray

Instructions:

- Please put all the ingredients in your blender's jar and mix them. Blend them up until they are completely pureed.
- While heating up, sprinkle some cooking spray onto the waffle iron.
- Cook the waffles for three to four minutes after pouring one cup of batter into each waffle mold.
- After it has been cooked, serve it with maple syrup and a fresh banana that has been diced up.

3.20 Veggies Cupcakes

Preparation time- 10 minutes | Cook time- 25 minutes | Servings- 24

Nutritional value- Calories- 127 | Fat- 5g | protein- 5g | Carbohydrates- 18g

Ingredients:

Cupcake liners

2 cups rolled oats

1 3/4 Cups whole-wheat pastry flour

1/4 cup chia seeds, ground

2 tbsp. baking powder

1 tsp baking soda

1 tsp cinnamon, ground

1/4 tsp nutmeg, ground

1/4 tsp allspice, ground

2 cups zucchini, shredded

1 cup canned pure pumpkin puree

1 cup of non-fat milk

4 large eggs, lightly beaten

1/4 cup unsweetened applesauce

1 tsp liquid stevia

Instructions:

- Preheat the oven to 375 degrees Fahrenheit and gas mark 5. Cupcake liners should be used to line two muffin pans that hold 12 muffins each. Set aside.

- Rolled oats, pastry flour, chia seeds, baking powder, baking soda, ground cinnamon, powdered nutmeg, and ground allspice should be combined in a large mixing basin before adding the other ingredients and combining well. Set aside.

- Mix the shredded zucchini, pumpkin puree, non-fat milk, beaten eggs, unsweetened applesauce, and liquid stevia in a second mixing dish of medium size.

- Mix the dry ingredients once the liquid components have been added. Mix in the cans that have been cut.

- Put about half of the batter into each of the cupcake liners. You may use a spoon or an ice cream scoop for this.

- Bake for another 25 minutes or until a toothpick inserted in the middle emerges clean.

- Allow the cupcakes to cool on a cooling rack for 5 minutes before removing them from the tins.

- Freeze any leftover cupcakes by wrapping them in plastic wrap beforehand. In the microwave, reheat the frozen cupcakes for twenty seconds once they have been removed.

Chapter 4 Vegetarian Recipes

4.1 Bean Wraps

Preparation time- 5 minutes | Cook time- 15 minutes | Servings- 2

Nutritional value- Calories- 115 | Fat- 34g | Protein- 20g | Carbohydrates- 21g

Ingredients:

- 2 tbsp green chili peppers, chopped
- 4 green onions, diced
- 1 tomato, diced
- 1 tbsp garlic, chopped
- 6 tortilla wraps, whole grain, and fat-free
- 3/4 cup cheddar cheese, shredded
- 3/4 cup salsa
- 1/2 cup corn kernels
- 3 tbsp cilantro, fresh and chopped
- 1/2 cup black beans, canned and drained

Instructions:

- In a bowl, combine the chili peppers, maize, black beans, garlic, tomato, onions, and cilantro.
- Microwave the mixture for one minute, then whisk for one minute.
- Spread the two tortillas between two paper towels and heat for 20 seconds in the microwave.
- Add ½ cup of the bean mixture to the remaining tortillas, 2 tablespoons of salsa, and 2 tablespoons of cheese.
- Roll them before serving.

4.2 Roasted Eggplant

Preparation time- 5 minutes | Cook time- 45 minutes | Servings- 8

Nutritional value- Calories- 89 | Fat- 7g | Protein- 1g | Carbohydrates- 7g

Ingredients:

- 1/4 cup of olive oil
- Fresh parsley and basil for serving
- 1/2 tsp. of garlic powder
- 2 large eggplants
- Salt
- 1 tsp. dried basil

Instructions:

- Using a knife, cut the eggplant in half along its length. Each half should be cut into four to six wedges.
- Salt the wedges and set them aside for 30 to 45 minutes.
- Preheat oven to 400 degrees Fahrenheit.
- Thoroughly rinse the eggplant and wipe it dry with paper towels. Coat the vegetables with olive oil and set them on a baking sheet.
- Use salt, pepper, and other ingredients to taste. Approximately 25 to 30 minutes, or until golden brown.

4.3 Balsamic Veggies

Preparation time- 5 minutes | Cook time- 30 minutes | Servings- 4

Nutritional value- Calories- 114 | Fat- 8g | Protein- 3g | Carbohydrates- 10g

Ingredients:

- 1 cup of grape tomatoes
- 8 ounces of mushrooms halved
- 1 cubed bell pepper
- 1 red onion cut into wedges
- 1 zucchini small sliced 1/2" thick

For the Marinade:

- 2 tsp. of balsamic vinegar
- 1 clove of minced garlic
- Salt & pepper to taste
- 2 tbsps. of olive oil

- 1 tbsp. Of chopped fresh rosemary

Instructions:

- All of the ingredients should be combined in a large mixing dish. Allow 30 minutes to eight hours of marinating time.

- Fire up the grill to a medium-high temperature.

- Place the veggies in a grilling basket after taking them from the marinade (or thread them onto skewers).

- Grill for about 8 to 12 minutes or until the desired doneness.

- Serve without delay.

4.4 Roasted Cauliflower

Preparation time- 5 minutes | Cook time- 20 minutes | Servings- 4

Nutritional value- Calories- 94 | Fat- 5g | Protein- 4g | Carbohydrates- 9g

Ingredients:

- 2 tsps. of olive oil

- 1/4 tsp. of sea salt

- 2 cups of chopped cauliflower florets

- 4 tbsps. of light raspberry vinaigrette

- 2 tbsp. of chopped walnuts

- 1/4 tsps. of black pepper

- 3 cups of mixed greens

Instructions:

- Set the oven temperature to 400 degrees Fahrenheit. Combine the cauliflower, olive oil, salt, and pepper. Roast for around 12 minutes in a preheated oven.

- Take the pan out of the oven and stir in the walnuts. Return to the oven for a further 5 minutes.

- Remove the baking dish from the oven and set it on a cooling rack. In the meanwhile, place the mixed greens in a salad dish. Add roasted cauliflower and nuts as a garnish.
- Before serving, combine all ingredients with the vinaigrette.

4.5 Broccoli Rabe

Preparation time- 10 minutes | Cook time- 0 minutes | Servings- 2

Nutritional value- Calories- 275 | Fat- 3g | Protein- 20g | Carbohydrates- 18g

Ingredients:

- 2 tbsps. of olive oil, divided
- 1 very thinly sliced garlic clove
- 3 tbsps. of water
- 1/4 tsp. of kosher salt
- 1 bunch of broccoli rabe, ends trimmed
- 1/4 tsp. of red pepper flakes

Instructions:

- Remove and then peel the broccoli rabe's thick bottom stalks.
- Put the blooms and foliage to one side.
- The oil should be heated over a medium-high temperature in a big pan.
- Add one tablespoon of olive oil, garlic, and red pepper flakes, and heat for about 45 seconds, or until the garlic and pepper flakes emit a pleasant aroma.
- Cook the stems for around 45 seconds or until the oil covers them.
- Pour in the water and continue boiling for another 3 to 4 minutes or until the stems are mostly tender.
- Combine the leaves, the flowers, and the salt. Cook with the cover on for 5 minutes or until the veggies are tender.
- Place the broccoli rabe and its liquids in a serving dish. One teaspoon of olive oil is sprinkled on the dish.

4.6 Fried Wok Veggies

Preparation time- 5 minutes | Cook time- 25 minutes | Servings- 8

Nutritional value- Calories- 79 | Fat- 5g | Protein- 4g | Carbohydrates- 7g

Ingredients:

- 2 pounds of bok choy - stalks halved & cut into 1/4-inch sticks
- 3 tbsps. of Chinese oyster sauce
- 2 tbsp. of vegetable oil
- 1 red bell pepper, seeded & cut into strips
- 1 tbsp. of minced fresh ginger
- 2 tbsps. of chopped cilantro leaves
- 3 cups of fresh bean sprouts
- 1/4 cup of Asian fish sauce
- 2 tbsps. of toasted sesame seeds
- 3 serrano Chile peppers, seeded & chopped
- 4 thinly sliced green onions

- 1/2 cup of baby corn, cut in half

Instructions:

- In a wok, bring the vegetable oil to a high temperature over a high burner. Stir the ginger and chilies into the oil after it has reached the desired temperature.

- Simmer and stir for thirty seconds or until the ginger releases a pleasant aroma.

- Mix in the baby corn, red pepper, and bok choy stalks until they are evenly distributed.

- Cook for approximately three minutes or until the texture of the red pepper has become more tender.

- After about one to two minutes, during which time you should mix the bok choy occasionally, it should have reached a dark green color and become wilted.

- Combine the oyster sauce, fish sauce, and chopped green onions in a mixing bowl.

- Mix in chopped cilantro and toasted sesame seeds just before serving.

4.7 BBQ Vegetables

Preparation time- 5 minutes | Cook time- 20 minutes | Servings- 5

Nutritional value- Calories- 175 | Fat- 11g | Protein- 3g | Carbohydrates- 14g

Ingredients:

- 2 cloves of garlic peeled & minced
- 1/4 cup of coarsely chopped fresh basil
- 3 sliced zucchinis
- 1 small eggplant, sliced into 3/4-inch-thick slices
- 6 fresh stems removed mushrooms
- 1/4 cup of lemon juice
- 2 small red bell peppers, seeded & cut into wide strips
- 1/4 cup of olive oil

Instructions:

- In a bowl of around medium size, combine the eggplant, zucchini, red bell peppers, and fresh mushrooms. Mix well.

- Using a whisk, combine the olive oil, basil, lemon juice, and garlic in a bowl of medium size.

- After spreading the sauce over the vegetables, cover the dish, and place it in the refrigerator for at least an hour so the flavors may meld.

- Raise the temperature on an outside grill to a high level.

- You may either skewer the veggies or place them on the grill to cook them.

- Cook for about two to three minutes on each side on a hot grill, basting with the marinade at regular intervals or until the meat is cooked to your satisfaction, whichever comes first.

4.8 Barley Lentil Soup

Preparation time- 15 minutes | Cook time- 50 minutes | Servings- 4

Nutritional value- Calories- 226 | Fat- 8g | Protein- 9g | Carbohydrates- 33g

Ingredients:

- 2 tbsp olive oil
- 2 carrots, peeled and chopped
- 1 large onion, chopped
- 2 celery stalks, chopped
- 2 garlic cloves, minced
- 1 tsp ground coriander
- 2 tsp ground cumin
- 1 tsp cayenne pepper
- 1 cup barley
- 1 cup red lentils

- 1 (14-oz.) can tomatoes, diced with liquid
- 8 cups of low-fat vegetable broth
- 4 cups of fresh spinach, torn
- Salt and ground black pepper, as needed

Instructions:

- Carrots, onion, and celery should be sautéed in oil that has been heated in a pot with a heavy bottom over medium heat for approximately five minutes.
- After approximately a minute of sautéing, add the garlic and the seasonings.
- To the pot, bring the broth to a boil, then stir in the barley, lentils, and tomatoes.
- Now reduce the heat to a low setting and continue to simmer the covered dish for around forty minutes.
- Simmer for approximately three to four minutes after adding the spinach, then season with salt and black pepper.
- To be served hot.

4.9 Mushroom Basil Soup

Preparation time- 10 minutes | Cook time- 30 minutes | Servings- 2

Nutritional value- Calories- 70 | Fat- 5g | Protein- 7g | Carbohydrates- 3g

Ingredients:

- 2 cups of tofu
- 1/3 cup of button mushrooms
- 1 cup of low-sodium vegetable broth
- 1 tsp of ginger powder
- 1 tsp of chopped fresh basil
- Olive oil to taste
- Salt to taste

Instructions:

- To begin, you will need to clean the button mushrooms, pat them dry, and then slice them after removing the earthy cap from the mushroom.

- After being washed and dried with a paper towel, the block of tofu should be sliced into cubes.

- Put one tablespoon of olive oil in a frying pan over medium heat. When the oil is heated, add the mushrooms, stir them, and continue cooking them for a couple of minutes until they brown.

- Next, pour in the vegetable stock and continue to boil for another 5 minutes; after that, stir in the ginger, crumbled tofu, and kosher salt.

- Continue to cook for another ten minutes with the lid on the pan.

- After ten minutes, turn off the heat and transfer the tofu and mushrooms to individual serving dishes.

- Serve immediately after sprinkling with the cooking juices and chopped basil.

4.10 Mixed Skillet

Preparation time- 10 minutes | Cook time- 15 minutes | Servings- 4

Nutritional value- Calories- 220 | Fat- 9g | Protein- 8g | Carbohydrates- 28g

Ingredients:

- ½ Cup Monterey Jack and Cheddar cheese blend, shredded

- 1 cup Uncooked instant white rice

- ¼ tsp. Dried oregano

- 4 cup Water

- 14.5 ounces Undrained fire-roasted diced tomatoes with garlic

- 15 ounces Rinsed and drained black beans

- ½ Cup Diced green bell pepper

- ½ Cup Chopped onion

- Small sliced zucchini
- 1 tbsp. Canola oil

Instructions:

- Place the oil in a big saucepan and bring it to temperature over medium heat.
- Once the saucepan has reached an appropriate temperature, put in the zucchini, bell pepper, and onion, and give the vegetables a chance to simmer for five minutes or until they have become more tender.
- Ensure that you stir them every so often while they are cooking.
- Stir in the oregano, the water, the tomatoes without the juice, and the beans.
- Raise the temperature slightly and wait until it reaches a full boil before proceeding.
- Fold in the rice while vigorously swirling the mixture to ensure that all flavors are evenly distributed.
- Cover the pan and remove it from the heat immediately after doing so.
- After the mixture has been combined, let it rest for seven minutes or until the rice has absorbed all the water.
- Generously sprinkle cheese over everything, and then dig in!

4.11 Wild Rice Salad

Preparation time- 10 minutes | Cook time- 20 minutes | Servings- 1

Nutritional value- Calories- 275 | Fat- 14g | Protein- 9g | Carbohydrates- 29g

Ingredients:

- 1/4 Cup wild rice, cooked
- ¼ Cup canned garbanzo beans, rinsed and drained
- 1 tsp basil pesto
- 1/4 cup canned corn, rinsed and drained
- ½ oz low-sodium feta cheese, crumbled
- 3 black olives, pitted and sliced

- 1/8 ripe avocado, peeled, pitted, and cut into slices
- Parsley, chopped for garnish (optional)
- Sea salt, fine
- Black pepper, ground

Instructions:

- Mix the cooked wild rice, garbanzo beans, and basil pesto in a dish of a more manageable size until everything is well combined.
- Spread the corn, feta, and olives in a uniform layer.
- Avocado and parsley should be used as garnishes (if using).
- Serve, and have fun with it!

4.12 Curried Veggies

Preparation time- 10 minutes | Cook time- 20 minutes | Servings- 8

Nutritional value- Calories- 131 | Fat- 2g | Protein- 6g | Carbohydrates- 23g

Ingredients:

- 4 tsp garlic, minced
- 1 tsp coconut oil
- 1 large yellow onion, chopped
- 1 medium red bell pepper, chopped
- 1 tbsp cumin, ground
- 1 tsp turmeric, ground
- 2 tsp smoked paprika
- ¼ tsp cayenne pepper
- ½ cup water
- 1 medium aubergine, cut into chunks
- 3 zucchinis, cut into chunks

- 3 medium tomatoes, diced

- 1 (15 oz) can of garbanzo beans, drained and rinsed

- ½ cup couscous

- 1 cup chicken broth

- Low-fat plain yogurt for garnish

Instructions:

- Place a big pan with a sturdy bottom over medium heat. Cook the minced garlic for one minute in the coconut oil. Add the chopped onion and pepper and cook for two to three minutes or until soft.

- Cook for one to two minutes after incorporating the ground cumin, turmeric, smoked paprika, and cayenne pepper.

- Add the water, aubergine, zucchini, tomatoes, and drained garbanzo beans. Reduce the heat to medium-low, cover, and cook for 15 minutes.

- Place the couscous and chicken broth in a small stockpot over medium heat while the veggies cook. Cover and bring the liquid to a boil.

- Reduce the heat to low and simmer for about 15 minutes until all the liquid is absorbed. Using a fork, remove the saucepan from the heat and fluff the couscous.

- Garnish the couscous with a dollop of plain yogurt and top with the curried veggies.

4.13 Spicy Tofu

Preparation time- 10 minutes | Cook time- 30 minutes | Servings- 5

Nutritional value- Calories- 134 | Fat- 7g | Protein- 10g | Carbohydrates- 9g

Ingredients:

1 tbsp olive oil

1 cup yellow onion, chopped

1 cup canned tomatoes, diced

½ cup sugar snap peas

1 tsp dried parsley

1 tsp chili powder

1 tsp cumin, ground

1/4 tsp sea salt, fine

1 cup tofu, crumbled

1 cup of water

8 tbsp cheddar cheese, shredded

Instructions:

- Warm the olive oil in a medium saucepan with a heavy bottom over medium heat.
- Constantly stirring, cook the chopped onion for 5 to 7 minutes until transparent.
- Add the chopped tomatoes with liquid from the can, sugar snap peas, dried parsley, chile powder, powdered cumin, and fine sea salt. Prepare for ten minutes.
- Add the crumbled tofu and water to the skillet and cook for ten minutes.
- Allow the chili mixture to boil until thickened for 5 to 10 minutes.
- The chili mixture should be topped with shredded cheddar cheese and served hot.

4.14 Zucchini Noodles

Preparation time- 20 minutes | Cook time- 20 minutes | Servings- 4

Nutritional value- Calories- 260 | Fat- 8g | Protein- 27g | Carbohydrates- 28g

Ingredients:

- Aluminum Foil
- 3 chipotle peppers, canned in adobo sauce
- 1 medium red bell pepper
- 1 banana pepper
- 1garlic clove, peeled
- ½ cup low-fat, plain yogurt
- 1 tbsp olive oil
- 1 tsp apple cider vinegar
- 1 tsp organic honey
- 1/2 lime, juiced

- ¼ tsp sea salt, fine
- ¼ tsp black pepper, ground
- 8 oz zucchini noodles

Instructions:

- Preheat the oven to 400 degrees Fahrenheit, gas mark 6. Wrap a baking sheet with aluminum foil.
- Place the chipotle pepper, bell pepper, banana pepper, and garlic clove on a baking sheet.
- Roast for 20 minutes, until soft.
- Roast the peppers and garlic for 20 minutes, turning once. Remove the food from the oven and let it cool.
- Remove the peppers' stems and seeds before cooking.
- In a food processor, combine the roasted peppers and garlic with plain yogurt, olive oil, apple cider vinegar, honey, lime juice, fine sea salt, and powdered black pepper until smooth.
- Fill a medium stockpot with water and boil the zucchini noodles for one to two minutes before draining them in a strainer.
- The zucchini noodles should be served with pepper sauce. Select the garnishes and serve.

4.15 Pinto Beans

Preparation time- 5 minutes | Cook time- 10 minutes | Servings- 4

Nutritional value- Calories- 121 | Fat- 1g | Protein- 7g | Carbohydrates- 20g

Ingredients:

- 1 tsp olive oil
- tsp garlic, minced
- (15 oz) can pinto beans, drained and rinsed

- 1 tbsp lime juice
- 1 tsp smoked paprika
- ½ tsp dried oregano
- ¼ tsp cayenne pepper
- ¼ tsp cumin, ground

Instructions:

- While the olive oil is warming in a small stockpot set over medium-low heat, add the garlic that has been minced and toss it around.

- Add the pinto beans that have been washed and continue to simmer for another 5 minutes until they are warm. Remove the pot from the heat.

- Whisk together the lime juice, smoked paprika, dried oregano, cayenne pepper, and ground cumin in a small bowl. Set aside.

- Coat the pinto beans with the lime juice mixture in a thorough manner.

- Place the bean mixture in a food processor and process it using the shredding blade until it becomes a purée.

Chapter 5 Poultry Recipes

5.1 Baked Potato Soup

Preparation time- 10 minutes | Cook time- 30 minutes | Servings- 6

Nutritional value- Calories- 181 | Fat- 9g | Protein- 9g | Carbohydrates- 18g

Ingredients:

- 4 slices turkey bacon (nitrate-free)
- 2 tbsps. extra-virgin olive oil
- 3 tbsps. whole-wheat flour
- 1½ cups 1% milk
- 1½ cups vegetable or chicken broth
- 3 medium unpeeled russet potatoes, cut into 1-inch chunks
- ½ cup low-fat plain Greek yogurt
- ½ cup shredded sharp Cheddar cheese
- 4 tbsps. chopped chives

Instructions:

- Put a large stockpot on the stove over medium heat. Add the bacon and fry until crispy on both sides, approximately 5 minutes, rotating once.
- Transfer to a plate lined with paper towels to absorb excess oil. After cooling, coarsely chop and put aside.
- In a stockpot, heat the olive oil over medium heat. Add the flour and cook, stirring for two to three minutes, until browned.
- Add the milk and continuously whisk until it begins to thicken. Whisk the broth in.
- Include potatoes. Reduce the heat to low and let the soup simmer for about 20 minutes or until the potatoes are cooked.
- Stir in the Greek yogurt to mix.

- Serve with turkey bacon, cheese, chives, and a dollop of plain Greek yogurt.

5.2 Creamy Chicken Soup

Preparation time- 15 minutes | Cook time- 40 minutes | Servings- 8

Nutritional value- Calories- 164 | Fat- 3g | Protein- 25g | Carbohydrates- 5g

Ingredients:

- 1 tsp minced garlic
- 1 tsp extra-virgin olive oil
- ½ yellow onion, diced
- 1 carrot, diced
- 1 celery stalk, diced
- 1½ pounds (3 or 4 medium) cooked chicken breast, diced
- 2 cups low-sodium chicken broth
- 2 cups water
- 1 tsp freshly ground black pepper
- 1 tsp dried thyme
- 2½ cups fresh cauliflower florets
- 1 cup fresh spinach, chopped
- 2 cups non-fat or 1% milk

Instructions:

- Put a large soup pot on the stove and turn the heat to medium-high. One minute of sautéing the garlic in olive oil should do the trick.
- Sauté the onion, carrot, and celery for three to five minutes or until the vegetables are soft.
- The chicken breast, broth, water, black pepper, thyme, and cauliflower should all be added at this point.

- Bring to a simmer, then turn the heat down to medium-low and continue cooking, uncovered, for another half an hour.

- After adding the fresh spinach and stirring it for approximately 5 minutes, it should have wilted.

- After stirring in the milk, the dish should be served right away.

5.3 Barley Veggie Chicken Soup

Preparation time- 15 minutes | Cook time- 50 minutes | Servings- 8

Nutritional value- Calories- 198 | Fat- 3g | Protein- 16g | Carbohydrates- 9g

Ingredients:

- 1 tbsp extra-virgin olive oil
- 1 tsp minced garlic
- 1 large onion, diced
- 2 large carrots, chopped
- 3 celery stalks, chopped
- 1 (14.5-ounce) can of diced tomatoes
- ¾ cup pearl barley
- 2½ cups diced cooked chicken4 cups low-sodium chicken broth
- 2 cups water
- ½ tsp dried thyme
- ½ tsp dried sage
- ¼ tsp dried rosemary
- 2 bay leaves

Instructions:

- Put a large soup pot on the stove and turn the heat to medium-high. Olive oil and garlic are heated together for one minute in a pan.

- Sauté the onion, carrots, and celery for three to five minutes or until the vegetables are soft.

- Add the tomatoes, barley, chicken, chicken broth, water, thyme, sage, rosemary, and bay leaves to the pot.

- Bring to a boil, immediately turn the heat down to medium-low and continue cooking, uncovered, for approximately half an hour. When the barley is soft, the soup is ready to be served.

- Please take out the bay leaves and throw them away before serving.

5.4 Grilled Chicken Wings

Preparation time- 15 minutes | Cook time- 20 minutes | Servings- 6

Nutritional value- Calories- 82 | Fat- 6g | Protein- 7g | Carbohydrates- 1g

Ingredients:

- 1½ pounds frozen chicken wings
- Freshly ground black pepper
- 1 tsp garlic powder
- 1 cup buffalo wing sauce, such as Frank's RedHot
- 1 tsp extra-virgin olive oil

Instructions:

- Bring the temperature of the grill up to 350 degrees Fahrenheit.
- Black pepper and garlic powder should be used to season the chicken wings.
- Cook the wings on the grill for 15 minutes on each side. When completed, they will have a browned appearance and a crisp texture.
- Mix the buffalo wing sauce with the olive oil, and then toss it with the grilled wings.
- Immediately serve after cooking.

5.5 Mexican Taco Skillet

Preparation time- 10 minutes | Cook time- 20 minutes | Servings- 6

Nutritional value- Calories- 162 | Fat- 7g | Protein- 18g | Carbohydrates- 8g

Ingredients:

2 tsp extra-virgin olive oil

1 large onion, finely chopped

1 tbsp minced garlic

1 jalapeño pepper, seeded and finely chopped

2 medium red bell peppers, diced

1 pound boneless, skinless chicken breast cut into 1-inch cubes

1 tbsp ground cumin

1 tsp low-sodium taco seasoning, such as from Penzeys Spices

1 (14.5-ounce) can of diced tomatoes

1 large zucchini, halved lengthwise and diced

½ cup shredded mild Cheddar cheese

1 cup chopped fresh cilantro

½ cup chopped scallions

Instructions:

- In a large skillet, heat the olive oil over medium heat. Add the garlic, onion, jalapeno, and red peppers. The veggies should be cooked for approximately 5 minutes or until tender.

- Stir in the chicken, cumin, and taco seasoning until the chicken and veggies are well-covered.

- Add the tomatoes and stir. Bring the ingredients to a boil. Reduce the heat to medium-low, cover the skillet, and simmer for 10 minutes.

- Mix in the zucchini well. Continue cooking for seven minutes or until the zucchini is soft.

- Take the pan away from the heat. Serve after combining the cheese, cilantro, and scallions.

5.6 Turkey Meatloaf

Preparation time- 10 minutes | Cook time- 50 minutes | Servings- 4

Nutritional value- Calories- 232 | Fat- 8g | Protein- 31g | Carbohydrates- 10g

Ingredients:

For the meatloaf

- Non-stick cooking spray
- 1 pound extra-lean ground turkey
- 1 large egg, lightly beaten
- ¼ cup whole-wheat bread crumbs
- ¼ fat-free feta cheese
- ¼ cup Kalamata olives pitted and halved
- ¼ cup chopped fresh parsley
- ¼ cup minced red onion
- ¼ cup plus 2 tablespoons hummus
- 2 tsp minced garlic
- ½ tsp dried basil
- ¼ tsp dried oregano

For the topping

- ½ small cucumber, peeled, seeded, and chopped
- 1 large tomato, chopped
- 2 to 3 tbsp minced fresh basil
- Juice of ½ lemon
- 1 tsp extra-virgin olive oil

Instructions:

To make the meatloaf

- Preheat the oven to 350 degrees Fahrenheit. Coat a loaf pan measuring 8 by 4 inches with cooking spray.

- Combine the turkey, egg, bread crumbs, feta cheese, olives, parsley, onion, and 2 tablespoons of hummus, garlic, basil, and oregano in a large bowl. With clean hands, thoroughly blend the ingredients.

- Evenly distribute the meatloaf ingredients in the loaf pan. Spread the remaining 14 cups of hummus on the meatloaf.

- Bake for 55 minutes.

To make the topping

- In a small bowl, combine the cucumber, tomato, basil, lemon juice, and olive oil. Refrigerate until serving time.

- The meatloaf is done when its internal temperature reaches 165 degrees Fahrenheit. Allow it to rest for 5 minutes before slicing and garnishing with the topping.

5.7 Zucchini and Turkey Meatloaf

Preparation time- 15 minutes | Cook time- 20 minutes | Servings- 4

Nutritional value- Calories- 191 | Fat- 5g | Protein- 22g | Carbohydrates- 15g

Ingredients:

- Non-stick cooking spray

- 1 tsp extra-virgin olive oil

- 1 large egg

- ½ cup whole-wheat bread crumbs

- ⅓ cup chopped onion

- 1-pound extra-lean ground turkey

- 1-pound zucchini

- ½ tsp freshly ground black pepper

- 2 cups Marinara Sauce with Italian Herbs

Instructions:

- Turn the oven up to 400 degrees Fahrenheit. Spray the bottom of a baking dish with a shallow depth with the cooking spray.

- Put the egg, bread crumbs, onion, and pepper into a big basin and mix them.

- Add the ground turkey and, using clean hands, thoroughly combine the ingredients until they are spread equally throughout the mixture.

- Form the beef mixture into balls about 2 inches in diameter, then set them in the baking pan.

- Bake the chicken for 15 minutes, uncovered.

- Remove the ends of the zucchini and set them aside. To make long, thin strips out of the zucchini, you may use a mandolin, a spiralizer, or the edge of a box grater.

- Warm up the olive oil in a pan of medium size at a heat setting of the medium.

- Sauté the zucchini strips for approximately 5 minutes or until they reach the desired level of tenderness.

- Place in a bowl that may be used for serving.

- Place the meatballs on top of the zoodles, and drizzle the marinara sauce.

5.8 Chicken Cordon Bleu

Preparation time- 15 minutes | Cook time- 30 minutes | Servings- 6

Nutritional value- Calories- 175 | Fat- 7g | Protein- 24g | Carbohydrates- 3g

Ingredients:

- Non-stick cooking spray
- 6 slices lean deli ham (nitrate-free)
- 6 boneless, skinless chicken breasts, thinly sliced
- 2 large eggs
- 1 tbsp. water
- 6 slices reduced-fat Swiss cheese, halved
- ¼ cup whole-wheat bread crumbs

- 2 tbsps. grated Parmigiano-Reggiano cheese

Instructions:

- Preheat the oven to 450 degrees Fahrenheit. Spray some cooking spray onto a baking sheet and set it aside.

- Pound the chicken breasts until they are a quarter of an inch thick.

- A piece of ham and a slice of cheese cut in half should be layered on top of each chicken breast.

- Roll the chicken around with caution.

- Position it on the baking pan with the seam-side down.

- In a low-sided basin, give the eggs a quick whisking.

- In a second, smaller bowl, combine the bread crumbs and Parmigiano-Reggiano cheese and stir well.

- Using a pastry brush, gently coat each chicken roll with the egg wash, and then sprinkle on the bread-crumb mixture before placing it in the oven.

- Bake the chicken for thirty minutes until it reaches an internal temperature of 165 degrees and has a golden brown crust.

5.9 Egg Roll

Preparation time- 10 minutes | Cook time- 20 minutes | Servings- 6

Nutritional value- Calories- 133 | Fat- 3g | Protein- 20g | Carbohydrates- 7g

Ingredients:

- 2 tsps. sesame oil divided

- 1 tsp. minced garlic

- 1 onion, finely diced

- 2 tsps. ground ginger

- pound extra-lean ground chicken or turkey

- 1½ tbsp. low-sodium soy sauce or Bragg Liquid Aminos

- ½ cup low-sodium beef broth
- ½ tsp. freshly ground black pepper
- 4 cups green cabbage, chopped or shredded into 1-inch ribbons
- 1½ cups shredded carrots
- 1 cup fresh bean sprouts or 1 (14-ounce) can be drained and rinsed
- 2 scallions, finely chopped, for garnish

Instructions:

- Put a big skillet on a burner that is set to medium-high heat.
- In addition to the garlic, add one teaspoon of sesame oil. Stir for 1 minute.
- After adding the onion, continue to sauté it for one to two minutes or until it is soft.
- Mix in the chicken that has been ground. Cook for 7 to 9 minutes, cutting the meat into smaller pieces as it cooks until it has browned.
- While the beef is browning, combine the remaining 1 teaspoon of sesame oil, the soy sauce, the broth, the ginger, and the black pepper in a small dish.
- After the chicken has finished cooking, pour the sauce into the frying pan and toss it.
- Include the bean sprouts, cabbage, and carrots in the dish. Stir to mix.
- Cook the cabbage over low heat with the lid on the skillet for about 5 to 7 minutes or until it is soft.
- Place in a bowl and top with scallions and more soy sauce to taste before serving.

5.10 Chicken with Mango Salsa

Preparation time- 15 minutes | Cook time- 60 minutes | Servings- 4

Nutritional value- Calories- 206 | Fat- 9g | Protein- 25g | Carbohydrates- 11g

Ingredients:

- 2 tbsps. extra-virgin olive oil
- 1 tsp ground ginger

- ¼ tsp cayenne pepper
- ½ tsp ground nutmeg
- Juice of 1 lime
- 1 tbsp. minced garlic
- ½ tsp dried thyme
- ½ tsp cinnamon
- 1 tsp freshly ground black pepper
- ½ tsp ground allspice
- 4 boneless, skinless chicken breasts about (1 pound chicken)
- ¼ tsp ground cloves
- 1 cup Mango Salsa

Instructions:

- Place the olive oil, lime juice, garlic, ginger, thyme, cinnamon, allspice, nutmeg, cayenne, cloves, and black pepper in a gallon-sized zip-top freezer bag.
- Shake the bag to combine the ingredients.
- After ensuring that the bag is completely sealed, carefully combine the marinade.
- To the marinade, add the chicken breasts and stir to coat. After ensuring the bag is sealed completely, shake it to evenly distribute the marinade over the chicken.
- Place in the refrigerator for at least half an hour or up to a full day.
- Prepare the grill by heating it to a medium-high temperature. After the chicken has been grilled, throw away the marinade and serve the chicken.
- Cook the chicken for about six minutes on each side or until the breasts have reached an internal temperature of 165 degrees Fahrenheit and the meat is no longer pink in the center.
- Alternately, the chicken may be baked in an oven warmed to 400 degrees Fahrenheit for approximately 25 minutes or until the juices are clear.

- Before slicing the chicken, let it rest for five minutes first. Spread some of the Mango Salsa on top of the chicken chunks.

Chapter 6 Sides and Snacks

6.1 Tuna Sandwich

Preparation time- 5 minutes | Cook time- 10 minutes | Servings- 3

Nutritional value- Calories- 250 | Fat- 3g | Protein- 20g | Carbohydrates- 25g

Ingredients:

- 3 lettuces leave
- 6 whole wheat bread slices
- ½ tsp of honey
- 1 tsp of mustard
- ¼ cup of low-fat vanilla yogurt
- 1 apple, peel and chop into small pieces
- 1 (6.5 ounces) can of tuna, packed in water, drained

Instructions:

- Place the apple pieces, tuna, mustard, honey, and yogurt in a dish of medium size. Mix well. Combine everything by stirring it.

- Place the bread pieces in a single layer on a level platter, then evenly distribute a half cup of the tuna mixture over each slice.

- On top of each, place a single leaf of lettuce and then cover it with another piece of bread.

6.2 Steak Fajita

Preparation time- 10 minutes | Cook time- 30 minutes | Servings- 4

Nutritional value- Calories- 186 | Fat- 10g | Protein- 8g | Carbohydrates- 10g

Ingredients:

- 1 tbsp of extra-virgin olive oil

- 1 medium yellow onion, slice into strips
- 1 red bell pepper, remove seed and cut into strips
- 1 yellow bell pepper, remove seed and cut into strips
- 2 tsp. minced garlic
- 1/2 lb. thin-cut steak cut into strips (Buy for pan frying)
- Salt and pepper to taste
- 1 tsp of cumin divided
- 1 tsp of coriander divided
- 1 tsp of chili pepper divided
- A pinch of cayenne pepper
- 4 cups of frozen cauliflower rice
- 2 tbsp of tomato paste
- 1/3 cup of water

Instructions:

- Cook the oil in a frying pan that has been preheated over medium heat until it is hot.
- Sauté the onion, garlic, and peppers for around five to seven minutes or until they have become softer.
- In the meanwhile, in a bowl, combine the steak strips with half of the cumin, half of the coriander, and half of the chili pepper.
- Season with salt and pepper to taste.
- Put the steak in the pan and cook it over medium heat until it's browned.
- After adding the cauliflower rice and stirring it, cook the dish for a few more minutes until the cauliflower rice has thawed.
- The remaining spices, along with the tomato paste, should be added. If it is too thick, add more water.
- Cover the pot and reduce the heat to low to medium.

- Cook over medium-high heat while stirring continuously for around 10–15 minutes. Try it out, then make any necessary adjustments to the seasonings.

- Chopped avocado, shredded cheese, and jalapeño peppers should be sprinkled on top.

6.3 Fruity Solace

Preparation time- 5 minutes | Cook time- 10 minutes | Servings- 8

Nutritional value- Calories- 79 | Fat- 1g | Protein- 3g | Carbohydrates- 17g

Ingredients:

- 2 cups of fresh cherries, strawberries, sliced bananas or ripe apple
- 1 tsp of vanilla extract
- 1/4 to 1/2 tsp of almond or spearmint extract
- 2 tbsp cornstarch
- 1/2 cup of sugar
- 1/2 cup of unsweetened cocoa
- 1 cup of cold coffee

Instructions:

- In a medium saucepan, whisk together the cornstarch, cocoa, coffee, and sugar until a thick consistency is achieved and bubbles begin to form.
- Remove the pan from the heat and stir in the extracts.
- Take bites of the fruit while dipping it in a cold or hot sauce.

6.4 Mashed Cauliflower

Preparation time- 10 minutes | Cook time- 5 minutes | Servings- 3

Nutritional value- Calories- 72 | Fat- 2g | Protein- 3g | Carbohydrates- 8g

Ingredients:

- 1 large head of cauliflower

- ¼ cup water
- ⅓ cup low-fat buttermilk
- 1 tbsp. minced garlic
- 1 tbsp. extra-virgin olive oil

Instructions:

- Create tiny florets from the cauliflower. Add the water to a large microwave-safe bowl.
- Cover and microwave cauliflower for about 5 minutes or until tender. Remove the liquid from the dish.
- Blend or process the buttermilk, cauliflower, garlic, and olive oil on medium speed in a blender or food processor until the cauliflower is smooth and creamy.
- Serve without delay.

6.5 Pickle Roll-ups

Preparation time- 20 minutes | Cook time- 0 minutes | Servings- 10

Nutritional value- Calories- 86 | Fat- 7g | Protein- 4g | Carbohydrates- 4g

Ingredients:

- ¼ pound deli ham thinly sliced
- 8 ounces Neufchâtel cheese at room temperature
- 1 tsp dried dill
- 1 tsp onion powder
- 8 whole kosher dill pickle spears

Instructions:

- You will need a big cutting board or a spot on a clean counter to put together your roll-ups.
- Place the ham slices on the work surface, and then apply the Neufchatel cheese in an even layer.

- Roll the ham gently around a pickle on one end of the meat.
- Cut each pickle roll-up into small rounds about half an inch wide.
- To make serving them more convenient, skewer each one with a toothpick.

6.6 Butternut Puree

Preparation time- 10 minutes | Cook time- 15 minutes | Servings- 8

Nutritional value- Calories- 78 | Fat- 3g | Protein- 5g | Carbohydrates- 6g

Ingredients:

- ⅛ tsp of cayenne pepper
- 1 tbsp of maple syrup
- 1 tbsp of butter
- 1-2 tbs of water
- 1 Butternut squash, seeds removed and peeled (cut into 1-inch cubes)

Instructions:

- Put the squash cubes in a dish that can withstand high temperatures and cover them with a paper towel.
- After five minutes in the microwave, remove the food and stir it.
- Cover once again and return to the microwave; continue cooking for 5 minutes or until the vegetables are tender; drain.
- Use a blender to puree the butternut squash, water, maple syrup, and cayenne pepper until the mixture is smooth.

6.7 Zucchini Fries

Preparation time- 10 minutes | Cook time- 0 minutes | Servings- 2

Nutritional value- Calories- 89 | Fat- 3g | Protein- 5g | Carbohydrates- 10g

Ingredients:

- 3 large zucchini

- 2 large eggs
- 1 cup whole-wheat bread crumbs
- ¼ cup shredded Parmigiano-Reggiano cheese
- 1 tsp. garlic powder
- 1 tsp. onion powder

Instructions:

- Prepare the oven to 425 degrees Fahrenheit. Prepare a big baking sheet with a rim by lining it with aluminum foil.
- After cutting each zucchini in half lengthwise, continue slicing it into fries approximately one and a half centimeters in diameter. You should get around 8 strips out of each zucchini.
- Break the eggs into smaller basins and give them a quick whisk.
- Mix the bread crumbs, Parmigiano-Reggiano cheese, garlic powder, and onion powder in a medium basin.
- After dipping each zucchini strip into the egg one at a time, roll them in the mixture of bread crumbs. Place on the baking sheet that has been prepared.
- Cook at a high temperature for 30 minutes, stirring the fries halfway during the cooking time. The zucchini fries are ready to be served when they are golden and crispy.
- Immediately serve after cooking.

6.8 Eggplant Pizzas

Preparation time- 15 minutes | Cook time- 30 minutes | Servings- 6

Nutritional value- Calories- 99 | Fat- 6g | Protein- 5g | Carbohydrates- 7g

Ingredients:

- 1 large eggplant, cut into ¼- to ½-inch rounds
- 1 tbsp. salt
- 1 tbsps. extra-virgin olive oil

- 2 tsps. minced garlic
- ½ tsp dried oregano
- 1 cup Marinara Sauce with Italian Herbs
- 1 cup fresh basil leaves
- 1 cup shredded part-skim Mozzarella cheese
- ¼ cup shredded Parmigiano-Reggiano cheese

Instructions:

- Prepare the oven to 425 degrees Fahrenheit. Prepare a big baking sheet with a rim by lining it with aluminum foil.

- Place the eggplant rounds on paper towels and then salt on both sides of each round. Allowing them to remain undisturbed for ten to fifteen minutes can assist in releasing some of the water that is contained inside the eggplant. Pat dry afterward. Removing all of the salt before beginning the baking process is unnecessary.

- Olive oil, garlic, and oregano should be combined and stirred in a separate dish.

- Arrange the eggplant circles on the baking sheet with a 1-inch gap between each one. Applying the olive oil and garlic mixture to each side of the eggplant with a pastry brush is highly recommended. Prepare the eggplant in the oven for fifteen minutes.

- On top of each cooked eggplant round, create pizzas by adding between one and two teaspoons of marinara sauce, two basil leaves, about one tablespoon of mozzarella cheese, and approximately one-half tablespoon of Parmigiano-Reggiano cheese.

- Continue baking the pizzas for another ten minutes or until the cheese is melted and beginning to color.

- Serve right away, and have fun with it!

6.9 Mixed Salad

Preparation time- 15 minutes | Cook time- 30 minutes | Servings- 4

Nutritional value- Calories- 75 | Fat- 4g | Protein- 2g | Carbohydrates- 8g

Ingredients:

- 1 large cucumber, seeded and sliced
- 4 medium tomatoes, quartered
- 1 medium red onion, thinly sliced
- ½ cup chopped fresh basil
- 3 tbsps. red wine vinegar
- 1 tbsp. extra-virgin olive oil
- ½ tsp. Dijon mustard
- ½ tsp. freshly ground black pepper

Instructions:

- Combine the tomatoes, red onion, cucumber, and basil in a bowl of medium size and stir well.
- Combine the vinegar, olive oil, mustard, and ground black pepper in a small bowl using a whisk.
- After pouring the dressing over the veggies, please give it a little swirl until everything is well distributed.
- Before serving, ensure the dish has been covered and chilled for at least thirty minutes.
- A suggestion for serving: Create a balanced meal from this salad.

6.10 Chipotle Hummus

Preparation time- 5 minutes | Cook time- 5 minutes | Servings- 2

Nutritional value- Calories- 52 | Fat- 2g | Protein- 2g | Carbohydrates- 6g

Ingredients:

- 1 (15.5-ounce) can of black beans, drained and rinsed
- Juice of 1 lime
- 1 chipotle pepper in adobo sauce

- 1 tsp. adobo sauce
- 1 tsp. minced garlic
- 2 tsps. ground cumin
- 2 tbsps. extra-virgin olive oil
- ¼ cup chopped fresh cilantro

Instructions:

- In a food processor or blender, pulse the black beans, lime juice, chipotle pepper, adobo sauce, garlic, cumin, olive oil, and cilantro on high for 2 to 3 minutes or until the mixture is extremely smooth.
- If the hummus is too thick, add 1 to 2 teaspoons of water to get the ideal consistency.
- Serve immediately or refrigerate for up to one week in an airtight jar.

Chapter 7 Beef & Pork Recipes

7.1 Pork Tenderloin Balsamic

Preparation time- 40 minutes | Cook time- 25 minutes | Servings- 4

Nutritional value- Calories- 175 | Fat- 4g | Protein- 23g | Carbohydrates- 3g

Ingredients:

- 1 pound of pork tenderloin
- 1 tsp of olive oil
- 1/2 tsp of cracked black pepper
- 2 1/2 tsp of coarse sea salt
- 2 tbsp of balsamic vinegar
- 4 garlic cloves

Instructions:

- Pour the mixture of olive oil, black pepper, balsamic vinegar, garlic, and salt over the meat. Marinate for at least thirty minutes or overnight if you have the time.

- Bring the oven to 400 degrees Fahrenheit.
- Over medium heat, brown the pork in a grill pan.
- Place pork browned in the oven and baked for 20 minutes.

7.2 Easy Meatloaf

Preparation time- 10 minutes | Cook time- 45 minutes | Servings- 6

Nutritional value- Calories- 84 | Fat- 10g | Protein- 31g | Carbohydrates- 3g

Ingredients:

- 1 tsp Italian seasoning
- 1 lightly beaten egg
- 1/4 cup of onion, finely chopped
- 1/4 cup of 2% mozzarella cheese, shredded
- 1/2 cup of grated parmesan cheese divided
- 1/2 cup of spaghetti sauce, divided
- 1 lb of lean ground beef

Instructions:

- Preheat the oven to 375 degrees. Combine 1/4 cup spaghetti sauce, meat, 1/4 cup mozzarella cheese, parmesan cheese, egg, onion, and seasonings.
- Spread the meat mixture in a dish measuring 12 by 8 inches.
- On top, sprinkle the remaining 1/4 cup of cheese and spaghetti sauce.
- Place in the oven and bake for 40 to 45 minutes until the internal temperature reaches 160 degrees Fahrenheit.

7.3 Black Bean with Pork Verde Stew

Preparation time- 15 minutes | Cook time- 55 minutes | Servings- 4

Nutritional value- Calories- 308 | Fat- 7g | Protein- 33g | Carbohydrates- 19g

Ingredients:

- 1 tsp of crushed red pepper flakes
- 1 (14.5 ounces) can of black beans, without salt, drained & rinsed
- 1 (14.5 ounces) can of diced tomatoes in juice (without salt)
- 1 (14-ounce) can of chicken broth (without salt)
- 1 packet Goya Sazon with coriander & annatto
- 1 tsp of ground cumin
- 2 cans of chipotle peppers in adobo sauce, minced + 1 tsp of adobo sauce
- 3 garlic cloves
- 1 cup of chopped onions
- 1 lb of pork tenderloin or loin, trimmed of visible fat and cut into 1-inch cubes
- 2 tsp of extra-virgin olive oil

Instructions:

- In a large saucepan, heat the olive oil over medium-high heat.
- Add the pork and simmer for four to six minutes, often stirring, until it is browned.
- Add the garlic and onion and continue cooking for two to three minutes or until the onion softens.
- Mix the cumin and chipotle chiles in adobo sauce and a spice package.
- Add chicken broth, beans, tomatoes, and red pepper flakes to the bowl (optional).
- Stir to mix ingredients. Bring mixture to a boil before reducing heat to low.
- Cover skillet and simmer over low heat for 45 to 60 minutes or until the port is cooked. Serve the stew over brown rice.

7.4 Beef Stir Fry

Preparation time- 15 minutes | Cook time- 15 minutes | Servings- 6

Nutritional value- Calories- 275 | Fat- 8g | Protein- 17g | Carbohydrates- 21g

Ingredients:

- 8-oz can of sliced water chestnuts
- 2 medium stalks of bok choy, cut into ½-inch slices
- ½ cup of instant brown rice
- ½ medium green, yellow or red bell pepper, cut into strips
- 3 oz of broccoli florets
- ¼ tsp of crushed red pepper flakes
- 1 tsp of canola oil
- 1 tbsp of cornstarch
- 3 tbsp of soy sauce
- ¼ (2 ounces) cup of hoisin sauce
- 6 oz beef broth (fat-free)
- 2 medium garlic cloves
- 2 tsp of ground ginger
- 1 lb of flank steak (cut into ¼-inch strips)

Instructions:

- Steak, ginger, and garlic should all be mixed in the mixing basin. Set aside.
- Cook the instant brown rice following the instructions provided in the box.
- Cornstarch, soy sauce, hoisin sauce, and broth should all be combined in the same dish. Stir the mixture until it is completely dissolved and properly blended.
- Bring the oil to a medium-high temperature in a pan, then add the red pepper flakes.
- After adding the steak, cook it while tossing it for about four to five minutes or until the meat is browned. Set aside.
- Carrot, red bell pepper, and broccoli should be added to the pan.

- Stirring constantly while cooking for two to three minutes over medium-high heat. (If the mixture becomes too dry, add 1–2 tablespoons of water.)

- Combine the water chestnuts and bok choy by stirring them in. Continue to cook for an additional one to two minutes, stirring often, or until the food is crisp-tender.

- Make a well in the center of the dish, then add the broth to the space you've created.

- Continue to cook for a further one or two minutes while swirling the mixture regularly until the broth becomes thicker.

- Mix in the ground beef and continue. Continue to cook for a few minutes until the food is completely heated. Serve on a bed of rice.

7.5 Chipotle Pork

Preparation time- 10 minutes | Cook time- 6 hours | Servings- 8

Nutritional value- Calories- 260 | Fat-11g | Protein- 20g | Carbohydrates- 5g

Ingredients:

- 1 (7.5-ounce) can of chipotle peppers in adobo sauce
- 1½ tbsps. apple cider vinegar
- 1 tbsp. ground cumin
- 1 tbsp. dried oregano
- Juice of 1 lime
- 2 pounds pork shoulder, trimmed of excess fat

Instructions:

- Blend or process the chipotle peppers and adobo sauce in a food processor or blender until smooth. Add the apple cider vinegar, cumin, oregano, and lime juice and mix well.

- The pork shoulder should be placed in the slow cooker, and the sauce should be poured over it.

- Turn the heat down to low, cover the slow cooker, and let it simmer for 6 hours.

- When the pork is done, it should be easy to shred. In the slow cooker, the pork should be shredded using two forks. If there is any sauce left over after the pork has been cooked, leave it to continue cooking on low for an extra 20 minutes so that it may absorb it.

7.6 Beef Stew

Preparation time- 15 minutes | Cook time- 40 minutes | Servings- 6

Nutritional value- Calories- 224 | Fat-10g | Protein- 17g | Carbohydrates- 13g

Ingredients:

- 4 tsps. extra-virgin olive oil, divided
- pound beef sirloin steak, cut into 1-inch cubes
- 2 tsps. minced garlic
- 1 medium onion, chopped
- pound rutabaga, cut into ½-inch cubes and peeled
- 3 medium carrots, cut into ½-inch cubes and peeled

- 1 small tomato, diced
- 1 tsp. smoked paprika
- ½ tsp. ground coriander
- ¼ tsp. red pepper flakes
- 2 tbsps. whole-wheat flour
- ½ cup red wine
- 3 cups low-sodium beef broth
- Fresh minced parsley, for garnish

Instructions:

- Warm up two tablespoons of olive oil in a big soup pot or Dutch oven and set the temperature to medium.
- After adding the beef, brown it on both sides by turning it often for approximately five minutes or until it is no longer pink. Place the mixture in a basin and put it aside.
- Over a medium heat setting, heat the two more teaspoons of olive oil in the same saucepan.
- After adding the garlic and onion, continue to sauté the mixture while turning it often for one to two minutes or until the onion is soft.
- Mix in the rutabaga, carrots, tomato, paprika, coriander, and red pepper flakes until everything is well distributed.
- After adding the flour, continue cooking for one minute while stirring the mixture.
- After adding the red wine, continue stirring for one more minute.
- After you've added the broth, put the meat back in the saucepan. Bring to a boil, and after it has reached a boil, decrease the heat to a simmer. The consistency of the sauce ought to start changing.
- Cook everything in the saucepan with the lid on for about half an hour or until all of the veggies are fork-tender.
- Parsley should be used as a garnish before serving.

Chapter 8 Desserts

8.1 Chocolate Chia Pudding

Preparation time- 15 minutes | Cook time- 60 minutes | Servings- 4

Nutritional value- Calories- 182 | Fat- 9g | Protein- 11g | Carbohydrates- 14g

Ingredients:

- 2 cups unsweetened soy milk
- 10 drops liquid stevia
- ¼ cup unsweetened cocoa powder
- ¼ tsp ground cinnamon
- ¼ tsp vanilla extract
- ½ cup chia seeds
- ½ cup fresh raspberries, for garnish

Instructions:

- Whisk the soy milk, stevia, cocoa powder, cinnamon, and vanilla together in a small bowl until all of the ingredients are well incorporated.
- Mix in the chia seeds well.
- Divide the mixture evenly among four smaller serving bowls.
- Cover and place in the refrigerator for at least an hour or overnight if you have the time.
- When you're ready to serve it, sprinkle some raspberries on top.

8.2 Peanut Butter Cookies

Preparation time- 15 minutes | Cook time- 15 minutes | Servings- 15 Cookies

Nutritional value- Calories- 275 | Fat- 8g | Protein- 17g | Carbohydrates- 21g

Ingredients:

- Nonstick cooking spray
- 1 cup natural smooth peanut butter
- 1 large egg
- ½ cup stevia baking blend
- ½ tsp. vanilla extract

Instructions:

- Turn the oven up to 350 degrees Fahrenheit. Spray some cooking spray onto a nonstick baking sheet, or use parchment paper instead.

- Put the peanut butter, egg, stevia, and vanilla in a bowl of medium size and mix them with a hand mixer.

- Form the batter into balls about 1 inch in diameter and lay them on the baking sheet. Reduce the thickness of each ball to about one-quarter of an inch.

- Create a crisscross design on the cookie using a fork to make two impressions in the dough.

- Cook for around 12 minutes. When they have reached the desired color, the cookies are finished.

- Allow cooling for 5 minutes before transferring to a baking rack to complete the cooling process.

8.3 Berry Custard

Preparation time- 5 minutes | Cook time- 35 minutes | Servings- 4

Nutritional value- Calories- 178 | Fat-3g | Protein- 13g | Carbohydrates- 21g

Ingredients:

- 1/4 tsp of nutmeg
- 1 cup blueberries
- 1 cup of raspberries
- 2 cups of non-fat evaporated milk
- 1/4 tsp of salt
- 1 tsp of vanilla extract
- 4 tsp of sugar substitute
- 2 large eggs
- 1 cup of water

Instructions:

- Preheat the oven to 350 degrees Fahrenheit. Spray an 8-by-8-inch baking dish with nonstick cooking spray.

- Pour one cup of water into a 9-by-13-inch baking dish and put it aside.

- Thoroughly combine the eggs, vanilla, sugar substitute, and salt; then add the milk and whisk.

- Blueberries and raspberries are combined and uniformly placed over the bottom of an 8-by-8-inch pan, followed by a custard/egg mixture layer.

- Insert the 8-by-8-inch baking dish into the 9-by-13-inch dish. (This prevents the custard from separating.)

- Bake the dish in the oven for 35 minutes. Insert a knife into the middle to see whether it's done; if it comes out clean, it's done. Remove the pan from the oven and sprinkle nutmeg on top.

8.4 Fruity Jelly Wrap

Preparation time- 10 minutes | Cook time- 0 minutes | Servings- 1

Nutritional value- Calories- 233 | Fat- 9g | Protein- 8g | Carbohydrates- 22g

Ingredients:

- 1/3 cup of fresh strawberries, sliced
- 1 tbsp of low-sugar strawberry jelly
- 3 tbsps. of regular ricotta cheese

- 1 small whole-wheat tortilla

Instructions:

- Strawberry jelly and ricotta cheese are spread over the tortilla. Add sliced strawberries on top.

- Serve the tortilla rolled up.

8.5 Peanut Butter Pancakes

Preparation time- 5 minutes | Cook time- 5 minutes | Servings- 4

Nutritional value- Calories- 233 | Fat- 9g | Protein- 8g | Carbohydrates- 22g

Ingredients:

- 1 cup frozen mixed berry blend
- 4 large egg whites
- 2 tbsp of powdered peanuts
- ½ cup of instant oatmeal
- ½ cup of low-fat cottage cheese

Instructions:

- Blend the cottage cheese, peanut powder, oats, and egg whites until the mixture is smooth.

- Transfer the berry mixture to a mixing bowl and gently fold it in.

- Spray your pan with cooking spray; pour about 1/4 cup of the batter into the skillet and heat, turning when the surface begins to bubble.

Chapter 9 30 Days Meal Plan

Sticking to a diet is a difficult challenge without a precise strategy.

Week 1

DAYS/MEALS	DAY 1	DAY 2	DAY 3	DAY 4	DAY 5	DAY 6	DAY 7
BREAK--FAST	Soymilk Shake	Soymilk Shake	Soymilk Shake	Vanilla Shake	Vanilla Shake	Vanilla Shake	Vanilla Shake

LUNCH	Soupy Chicken	Pea Pottage	Hearty Tomato	Chicken Squash	Creamy Carrot Soup	Super Soup	Fried Beans
DINNER	Creamy Carrot Soup	Super Soup	Classic Tuna Salad	Chicken Salad	Soupy Chicken	Pea Pottage	Hearty Tomato

Week 2

DAYS/MEALS	DAY 1	DAY 2	DAY 3	DAY 4	DAY 5	DAY 6	DAY 7
BREAK-FAST	Apple Pie Shake	Peanut Butter Cup Shake	Peach Smoothie	Apple Avocado Juice	Cinnamon Chiller	Fruits Oats	Pumpkin Latte
LUNCH	Beef Stew	Chipotle Pork	Pinto Beans	Wild Rice Salad	Mushroom Basil Soup	Broccoli Rabe	Bean Wraps
DINNER	BBQ Vegetables	Zucchini Noodles	Barley Lentil Soup	Baked Potato Soup	Egg Roll	Spicy Tofu	Curried Veggies

Week 3

DAYS/MEALS	DAY 1	DAY 2	DAY 3	DAY 4	DAY 5	DAY 6	DAY 7
BREAK-FAST	Chicken Tart	Radish Hash	Bacon Eggy Bites	Savory Soufflé'	Salmon Bruschetta	Veggies Cupcakes	Acorn Squash
LUNCH	Roasted Cauliflower	Grilled Chicken Wings	Mixed Skillet	Chicken with Mango Salsa	Mashed Cauliflower	Mexican Taco Skillet	Creamy Chicken Soup
DINNER	Pinto Beans	Fried Wok Veggies	Balsamic Veggies	Roasted Eggplant	Bean Wraps	Turkey Meatloaf	Chicken Cordon Bleu

Week 4

DAYS/MEALS	DAY 1	DAY 2	DAY 3	DAY 4	DAY 5	DAY 6	DAY 7
BREAK-FAST	Apple Pie Shake	Peanut Butter Cup Shake	Peach Smoothie	Apple Avocado Juice	Cinnamon Chiller	Fruits Oats	Pumpkin Latte

LUNCH	Beef Stew	Chipotle Pork	Pinto Beans	Wild Rice Salad	Mushroom Basil Soup	Broccoli Rabe	Bean Wraps
DINNER	BBQ Vegetables	Zucchini Noodles	Barley Lentil Soup	Baked Potato Soup	Egg Roll	Spicy Tofu	Curried Veggies

Week 5

DAYS/MEALS	DAY 1	DAY 2
BREAK--FAST	Chicken Tart	Radish Hash
LUNCH	Roasted Cauliflower	Grilled Chicken Wings
DINNER	Pinto Beans	Fried Wok Veggies

Conclusion

The diet will evolve over one year. Beginning with two to four weeks on a liquid diet consisting of protein drinks and water. You will gradually transition to soft solid meals. You should be able to consume typical foods, such as cheese, eggs, and shellfish, after around two months. Your recommended daily caloric intake is around 500 calories. You will consume around 70 grams of protein, 30 grams of fat, and 40 grams of carbs daily. In the first year, your caloric intake will rise, and most individuals will have met their weight reduction objectives and be able to consume between 900 and 1,500 calories per day. Your calories will depend on your activity level, gender, and age. Men are permitted to consume more calories.

Thank you for making it to the conclusion of Bariatric Surgery; we hope it was helpful and provided you with all the resources you need to accomplish your objectives, whatever they may be. If you believe bariatric surgery is correct, you should see your physician. If you have previously had the procedure, then begin experimenting with these recipes. Finally, you can access many recipes if you are scheduled for surgery.

Printed in Great Britain
by Amazon